No Greater Monster nor Miracle than Myself

THE McDONALD
CENTER FOR
AMERICA'S FOUNDING
PRINCIPLES

MERCER
UNIVERSITY

The A.V. Elliott Conference Series

The Thomas C. and Ramona E. McDonald Center
for America's Founding Principles

Guided by James Madison's maxim that "a well-instructed people alone can be permanently a free people," the McDonald Center exists to promote the study of the great texts and ideas that have shaped our regime and fostered liberal learning.

Directors
Will R. Jordon
Charlotte C. S. Thomas

NO GREATER MONSTER NOR MIRACLE THAN MYSELF

The Political Philosophy of Michel de Montaigne

Charlotte C. S. Thomas, Editor

MERCER UNIVERSITY PRESS
MACON, GEORGIA

MUP/ P487

Based on the March 2012 conference sponsored by
Mercer University's Center for America's Founding Principles

Published 2014 by
Mercer University Press
1400 Coleman Avenue
Macon, Georgia 31207

9 8 7 6 5 4 3 2 1

Books published by Mercer University Press are printed on acid-free paper that meets the requirements of the American National Standard for Information Sciences—Permanence of Paper for Printed Library Materials.

Library of Congress Cataloging-in-Publication Data

No greater monster nor miracle than myself : the political philosophy of Michel de Montaigne / edited by Charlotte C.S. Thomas.
pages cm
Includes bibliographical references and index.
ISBN 978-0-88146-485-6 (pbk. : alk. paper) -- ISBN 0-88146-485-6 (pbk. : alk. paper)
1. Montaigne, Michel de, 1533-1592. I. Thomas, Charlotte C. S., editor of compilation.
B785.M74N6 2014
194--dc23

2014000361

Contents

Acknowledgments

This collection of essays is based on the 5th annual conference on Great Books and Ideas sponsored by Mercer University's McDonald Center for America's Founding Principles (formerly, The Center for the Teaching of America's Western Foundations), so it owes great debts not just to those who have made this volume possible, but also to all of those who helped make that conference an occasion for such a lively and thoughtful inquiry into Montaigne's *Essays*.

The McDonald Center for America's Founding Principles was created by Matthew Oberrieder and Will Jordan and supported in 2008 by Mercer University's Academic Initiatives fund. Neither the conference on Montaigne in March 2012, nor any of the other excellent programs sponsored by the Center would have been possible without the foresight of President William D. Underwood, the confidence of the Academic Initiatives committee, the support of Lake Lambert, Dean of the College of Liberal Arts, or the entrepreneurial spirit of Drs. Oberrieder and Jordan.

In the spring of 2013, the Center received a generous endowment gift from A.V. Elliott, for whom our annual conference is now named. Thomas C. and Ramona McDonald then made a significant endowment gift in late 2013, and have given their name to our Center. We are deeply in debt to the McDonalds and Elliotts for their support of our programs and the great confidence they have shown in our work.

Our conference on the Political Philosophy of Montaigne was both a gathering of Montaigne scholars and the culmination of a semester long reading group made up of Mercer faculty and students. I would like to thank all of the participants in that group by name. Each of them contributed significantly both to my growing appreciation for the subtlety of Montaigne's thought and to the liveliness of our conference. So, thank you: Will Jordan, Tom Huber, Randy Harshbarger, Kevin Cummings, Bryan Whitfield, Mary Ann Drake, Natalie Bourdon, Deneen Senasi, Patrick Jolley, Sarah Wibell, Josh Coleman, Cameron Kunzelman, James Hedgis, Catherine Roe, Hunter Pilkington, and Tyler Bishop.

My deepest thanks go out to Ann Hartle, John Scott, Daniel Cullen, Christine Henderson, Eduardo Velasquez, Kevin Honeycutt, and Christopher Edelman, who came to Mercer to present their work on Montaigne at our conference in March of 2012. Their scholarly work was serious and provocative, and they all gave generously of their time and talents to make our three days together remarkably enjoyable and productive. I would also like to thank our student panelists at the conference: Joseph Clark, Avani Patel, Nand Patel, and Andaika Jean-Noel for their good work and great courage.

Many thanks are due to Mercer University Press and, especially to its director, Marc Jolley, who has been extremely helpful and supportive throughout the process of publishing this volume.

Thanks also to Randy Harshbarger for his help with the French Translation.

Finally, it has been my privilege to work as Co-Director of the McDonald Center for America's Founding Principles for the past three years. I have had the remarkable opportunity to promote serious conversation about liberal learning and its influence on the American founding, while creating incredible learning opportunities for my students and developing new friendships and collegial conversations with people I would otherwise be likely never to meet. But the greatest part of that privilege has been working with my Co-Director, Will Jordan, who brings wisdom, prudence, and kindness to everything he does.

Introduction

Montaigne begins his book with *Au Lecteur*, "To the Reader,"[1] and thus with a few famously important claims about the nature of his *Essais*. First, he tells us that the book was written" in good faith" and that its goals are purely "domestic and private," neither oriented toward rendering service to the reader, nor garnering glory for the writer. But, with these caveats in place, Montaigne moves immediately to an account of at least one purpose that he hopes the book will serve. "I have dedicated it to the private convenience of my relatives and friends, so that when they have lost me (as soon they must), they may recover here some features of my habits and temperament, and by this means keep the knowledge they have had of me more complete and alive." The book may not have been written with public goals, but it is not simply private or self-serving either. After Montaigne has died, it will serve those who loved him by keeping his habits and temperament in the world. Those who would have been his friends, had they not been separated from Montaigne by space and time, may also be served by his book. In that way, the form of the *Essays* offers a new sort of life for Montaigne.

This book of essays collects papers presented at the Fifth Annual A.V. Elliott Conference on Great Books and Ideas sponsored by Mercer University's McDonald Center for America's Founding Principles in March 2012. Its ambitions

[1] All references to the French text of the *Essais* are to the edition by Maurice Rat (Paris: Gallimard, 1962) . English translations of Montaigne come from *The Complete Essays of Montaigne*, trans. Donald Frame (Stanford: Stanford University Press 1958).

are less expansive and lofty than those of Montaigne's book, but some are similar. If those who attended that conference recognize it in this book, then this volume will be a success. If the book reaches out to those who would have enjoyed the company of those who gathered then, but who could not be there, even better.

Alive, Montaigne had defects and acted imperfectly. That is to say, he was human. In order to make himself recognizable in the book, he portrays himself without omitting those aspects of his life and character that exhibit his shortcomings. Had he "written to seek the world's favor," he would have "bedecked [himself] better," presented himself "in a studied posture" (*To the Reader* (3), but it is not the world's favor that he seeks. Instead, Montaigne works to leave a living version of himself behind for his friends. He wants to be recognizable in the book. The ambition to make himself recognizable, however, is not identical to the ambition to garner recognition, at least not public recognition. He is not writing for those who cannot or will not recognize him.

Montaigne does not seek the world's favor in the *Essays,* but he has written his book to be read. He presents to his readers a living, breathing, body of work—one in which his life will be recognizable to his friends and through which he will continue to live on for them. So, the book has no overtly public functions, but neither is it a private journal. Instead, it will translate his character into a form that will not die when he does. He is the matter of his book, and he has sought not to leave it to the world uninformed.

How does Montaigne set out to write a living book, a substantial book? He writes his life not as if he were sitting for a portrait, but from nature—in motion, with flaws, in flux, and not bound to the laws of non-contradiction. He will not adopt the rigid posture of one sitting for a painted portrait, but he will also not avoid completely a concern for those who may view him in the book. He cannot, he tells us with some apparent remorse, portray himself naked. He would, if he could, but he cannot because his "respect for the public" implies certain boundaries for his presentation of himself. Nakedness is important to Montaigne because it stands in for a version of nature that is not natural to him. He will neither portray himself in the studied posture of one seeking the world's favor, nor as one who lives "still in the sweet freedom of nature's first laws." There are some customs that Montaigne can and will forego and others that he will not, perhaps because he cannot. Such a presentation of himself, stripped of every bit of culture and custom would be no more accurate than the posed portrait that neglects almost everything but custom. Montaigne neither gives himself wholly to custom, nor does he pretend to withdraw from it entirely. To be recognizable to those who knew him, and perhaps to himself, Montaigne needs to show himself neither in a studied posture nor in an unclothed form, but in the in-between mode that he inhabited in life.

According to Ann Hartle's contribution to this volume, "Montaigne's Invention of Society," Montaigne's *Essays* inhabit the social space between the public and the private so profoundly that they invent a new mode of human association. "The invention of the essay is the invention of society, for the essay is the unprecedented revelation of a merely private, common man who emerges into the public with no great deeds to tell." This is not to say that she argues that "men did not engage in activities that we regard as social or that they were not "sociable," before Montaigne's *Essays*. "It is to say that society did not exist as a recognized third mode of association with boundaries and freedoms of its own." Society, as a shared realm inhabited by voluntarily associated friends, is the realm defined neither by seeking public approbation nor by solitude. It is that mode of human association built on voluntarism and trust, or the realm where intimacies, confessions, and *essais* belong.

Christopher Edelman's essay, "Belonging to Oneself: Montaigne and Moral Autonomy," explores Montaigne's account of himself as self-governing, subject to his own laws and judgments. Montaigne's understanding of autonomy differs both from Plato before him and from Kant to follow. "It is not simply that Montaigne is not interested in pursuing Platonic self-mastery. For in addition to his lack of interest in self-mastery, Montaigne calls into question the moral authority of reason, and in doing so he challenges both the Platonic and the Kantian conceptions of autonomy." The nature of Montaigne's autonomy and his pursuit of it are expressed in his "essaying" activity, for it is in that endeavor that Montaigne discovers, constitutes, judges, legislates, and governs himself.

In "'Being a Citizen of No City': The Essais and the Political," Christine Dunn Henderson asks three provocative questions: (1) What kind of guidance does Montaigne offer us about good political life?; (2) What type of regime would be most conducive to Montaigne's?; and (3) What would a regime of Montaigne's look like? Montaigne explicitly distances himself from politics, but this distancing itself and Montaigne's reasons for it illuminate the boundaries of the political as he sees them. One implication is that in a Montaignian regime it should be possible to distance yourself from public life. The regime would be modern in the sense of privileging the individual over the community, at least insofar as is necessary for public service to be voluntary. Moderation, rule of law, and freedom of religion, among other things emerge, by implication, as characteristics of political orders Montaigne could affirm and thrive within. The foundations of true friendship—openness, trust, and mutual pleasure—would also be the foundational principles of Montaigne's regime, an order built on and around the possibility of political friendship among its citizens.

In "How to Get Drunk: A Practical Guide for the Perplexed (Or, on Michel de Montaigne's 'Of Drunkeness')," Eduardo Velasquez reminds us that "Michel de Montaigne's *Essays* are as up-to-date as anything we can scroll through on the front page of the *New York Times* or graze on Academic.com's 'cutting edge research.'" Immersed in, formed by, and thinking through culture, Montaigne manages to find himself, and so can we. "He bears witness to the possibility that we are more than the accretions of a fragmentary cultural inheritance ingested indiscriminately." In order to follow Montaigne's path, we must "essay" what we ingest; we must, among other things, learn how to get drunk, and on what. No doubt, Montaigne's essay "Of Drunkenness" is partially about inebriation on fermented beverages, but it is also about his father, promiscuity, Stoicism, and philosophy. "Drunkenness is Montaigne's metaphor for that loosening of self that makes us tolerable to ourselves and open to the individuality of another." Drunkenness is among the basest and broadest human actions, and "essaying" it, as with so many other human things, sounds out the profound depths and aspirations for Montaigne's examined life, and perhaps ours.

Kevin Honeycutt's essay, "Eschatological Dissatisfaction: Montaigne's Response to Machiavelli on Fortune and Death," explores the resonances between Machiavelli and Montaigne's treatment of fortune and implications for each philosopher's understanding of a proper human comportment to mortality. Machiavelli's *Prince* famously considers fortune as a condition to which all human life is subject, and he advises princes to learn how to use cruelty and deception in order to conquer it. Far from recommending cruelty and deception, Montaigne singles them out as particularly loathsome vices. He suggests not only that we use different means to respond to fortune, but also that we pursue different ends in relation to it. "Montaigne says that we should be grateful when fortune puts us to the test. But it is more praiseworthy to seek out fortune and put her to the test, as did Epaminondas, Socrates, and the Stoics and Epicureans." While Machiavelli seeks to master fortune and, by analogy, death, Montaigne strives to "essay" himself against it.

Daniel E. Cullen looks forward from Montaigne to Rousseau in "Montaigne and Rousseau: *Ou, Les Solitaires*." Montaigne and Rousseau come to their solitude by different paths: Montaigne chooses retirement and Rousseau, by the time he writes *Reveries of a Solitary Walker*, has been excluded from French intellectual society against his will. Both thinkers, however, embark on a project of self-authorship made possible by their solitude. The differences and similarities between Montaigne and Rousseau's ambitions and accomplishments on the path toward self-authorship get to the core of the shared philosophical concerns. These shared concerns turn Montaigne toward his tower or an *arriere boutique*, that is toward a retirement that does not draw itself entirely away from activity and the world. The same shared concerns send Rousseau in pursuit of "that way station between being and non-being" he calls "reverie."

Together, the essays in this volume explore the shared private space that Montaigne creates with the *Essais*. Montaigne does not withdraw from the world when he retires, although he clearly removes himself from political and public responsibility beyond the boundaries of his estate. He inhabits a private space and invites those who can to join him. During his lifetime, this invitation was narrowly extended and, notably in the case of Etienne la Boetie, did not always work out. But, through the *Essais*, Montaigne makes himself available to be brought into society with us. He is the matter of his book, and he lives on in it, recognizable to those who know him. When we read the *Essais*, especially when we read them together as we did at Mercer in 2012, we keep company with this great man. And, if we take the responsibilities of our society with Montaigne seriously, we cannot help but be elevated, at least just a bit, by his company.

1

Montaigne's Invention of Society

Ann Hartle

Montaigne "invents" society, the new, distinctly modern form of human association that serves as the limit on the power of the state. The invention of the essay is the invention of society, for the essay is the unprecedented revelation of a merely private, common man who emerges into the public with no great deeds to tell. The social rather than the political realm becomes the place for the pursuit of the human good. Montaigne's treatment of marriage, friendship, freedom of speech, liberal education, and religion display a coherent picture of the goods pursued in a free society and of the character that is required for the pursuit of those goods.

As Hannah Arendt explains, for the ancient and, in some ways, even for the medieval world, only two spheres of human association existed, the private realm of the household and the public realm of political life. The private is hidden because the actions of private life are those that are merely necessary, that is, unfree or servile, for they are associated with mere life. Modern society comes into existence when the private realm emerges into the public. To say that society is a new kind of association is not to say that men did not engage in activities that we regard as social or that they were not "sociable." It is to say that society did not exist as a recognized third mode of association with boundaries and freedoms of its own. The private realm of the household had been seen in pre-modern times as imperfect and incomplete because the most significant human goods could be pursued only in the political realm. The invention of society entails nothing less than the re-location of the good to the social rather than the political sphere of life.

Montaigne "invents" society. He actually brings it into existence through the publication of his *Essays.* The meaning of 'invention' in the sixteenth century was 'discovery', but discovery, in this sense, entailed the act of bringing something to light and thereby actually bringing it into existence: if it were not brought into the light, it would not have a recognizable identity. It could not come into existence on its own, naturally, without human intervention. The new is what was always there, but hidden. For Montaigne, society is implicit or intimated in the domestic and private.

Montaigne tells us, in the very first words of his preface to the reader, that his "end" in this work is "domestic and private" (F2).[1] Society, as Arendt shows, is the domestic and private brought out into the public. And that is precisely the action of the *Essays*: Montaigne writes about himself, a merely private man with no great deeds to boast of, revealing in public the hidden, intimate details of his private life.

Society is a third, entirely new, distinctly modern form of human association that is public but not political. As Arendt says: "The emergence of society…from the shadowy interior of the household into the light of the public sphere, has not only

---

[1] The English translation of the *Essais* is that of Donald Frame, *The Complete Essays of Montaigne* (Stanford, Calif.: Stanford University Press, 1943). The French text of the *Essais* in the edition by Pierre Villey and V. L. Saulnier, 3 vols., 2nd edition (Paris: Universitaires de France, "Quadridge," 1992, and in some instances, I have emended Frame's translation. I have also consulted the translation by M. A. Screech, *The Essays of Michel de Montaigne* (London: Penguin Press, 1991).

blurred the old borderline between private and political, it has also changed almost beyond recognition the meaning of the two terms and their significance for the life of the individual and the citizen."[2]

Michael Oakeshott describes the momentous changes that were taking place during Montaigne's lifetime: "During the late fifteenth and sixteenth centuries, governments all over Europe were, in varying degrees, acquiring a power to control the activities and destinies of their subjects such as their predecessors had never enjoyed." Now "the tireless, inquisitive, roving hand of government was beginning to be able to reach everywhere, accustoming the subject to the notion that nothing should be beyond its grasp." According to Oakeshott, "the most significant of all these changes was...the gradual disappearance of the intermediate authorities which had formerly stood between a then weak central government and the subjects, leaving them naked before a power which in its magnitude was becoming comparable to a force of nature."[3]

At the same time, the standards of pre-modern political life were being called into question by early modern political philosophers. For pre-modern politics, the most basic principle, the standard by which a political entity must be judged, is "the common good." The common good is not simply a good that we as individuals all want, e.g., food and shelter, but a good that can only be pursued and enjoyed in common. For Plato, Aristotle, and the medieval tradition, that good is moral virtue, especially justice. Cities in which rule was exercised for the

[2] Hannah Arendt, *The Human Condition* (Chicago: University of Chicago Press, 1958) 38.

[3] Michael Oakeshott, *The Politics of Faith and the Politics of Scepticism*, ed. Timothy Fuller (New Haven: Yale University Press, 1996) 76.

common good were judged to be just while those in which rule was exercised for the benefit of the rulers were judged to be unjust. The human good, at least in this world, could be achieved only in the political realm. Early modern political philosophers such as Machiavelli reject the common good as the goal of politics, judging it to be an impossible standard, never actually achieved in practice.

Montaigne also rejects the standard of the common good. As Oakeshott says, "Montaigne has no illusions about human power."[4] His mistrust of the use of power explains why he sees the principle of the common good as "the pretext of reason" for the actions of vicious men: it is possible to justify all kinds of evil, violence, and cruelty in the name of the common good (III:1,609-10). Therefore, Montaigne says that, "since philosophy has not been able to find a way to the good that is good in common, let each one seek it in his particularity!" (II:16,471). This freedom of the individual to pursue the good in his own way is one of the fundamental principles of modern politics.

The common good was, in principle, the check on the power of government, for the ruler was to be held to the standard of moral virtue. With the disappearance of the standard of the common good, based on realism concerning the human propensity for evil, the best that can be sought in the public realm is the limitation of evil. In her "Méditation sur l'obéissance et la liberté," Simone Weil concludes that the formula of "the least evil" is the only one applicable in the political realm. The struggle between those who command and those who obey is inevitable and can only be suppressed by

---

[4] Ibid., 49.

constraint. Therefore, the limitation of violence is the best that can be done by those who love liberty.[5]

But given the expansion of the power of government and the elimination of intermediate authorities as described by Oakeshott, the limitation of that power becomes extremely difficult. So, for example, Hobbes concludes that it is impossible to impose limits on the sovereign without incurring the risk of civil war. Montaigne says of the power of the prince: "It is difficult for a power so unmeasured to observe measure" (III:7,700).

I. The Invention of Society.

In "Of custom" Montaigne tells us that, at one time, he had found himself in the position of having to justify an authoritative customary observance, an observance that he does not identify. He wanted to establish this custom, not simply by the force of the laws and examples, but by tracing it back to its origin. But in doing so, he discovered that its "foundation" was "so weak" that he, who was supposed to justify it to others, instead became "almost disgusted" by this practice (1:23,84). When the mask of custom is torn off, the authority of the practice is exposed as based on nothing but time and usage; and when Montaigne subsequently measures custom by the standard of truth and reason, his judgment is "all upset" but "nevertheless restored to a much surer status" (I:23,84-85). How can his judgment be "restored" once he has seen the weak origin of custom?

---

[5] Simone Weil, "Méditation sur l'obéissance et la liberté," in Etienne De La Boétie, *Le Discours de La Servitude Volontaire. La Boétie et la Question du Politique*, (Paris: Payot, 1985) 95.

The examples he uses to show what happens to him in his attempt to rid himself of the prejudice of custom illustrate the strangeness and even barbarity of French laws: they illustrate the way that judgment is upset when one refers custom to truth and reason. What could be more strange, he asks, than to see a people governed by laws it does not understand, that is, laws written and published in Latin, which therefore require paid interpreters? It is "monstrous" that reason, law, and justice must be bought and sold. What could be more barbarous than the simultaneous existence of two codes of conduct: the code of arms, which binds the nobility by the standard of honor, and the civil code, which forbids the avenging of insults? "There are two sets of laws, those of honor and those of justice, in many matters quite opposed. The former condemn as rigorously a man's enduring being given the lie as the latter condemn his avenging it." He asks, "what could be more barbarous" than the condition in which a man is degraded from honor and nobility if he endures an insult without avenging himself and incurs capital punishment if he does avenge himself? (I:23, 85)

Immediately after the discussion of these strange and barbarous customs, he turns to consider more "indifferent things," such as clothing. Just as there are monstrous laws, so also there are monstrous fashions in clothing, monstrous because they do not serve the needs and comfort of the body "on which depend their original grace and fitness." It is possible, then, that someone would "want to restore them to their true end" (I:23,85). By turning to indifferent things, Montaigne suggests that in a similar way custom and the laws might also be restored to their true end.

Further, within the discussion of strange and monstrous laws, there are suggestions of other possibilities. With respect to the burdens imposed by the Latin laws, which bind the people in all of their domestic affairs and which must be interpreted by paid lawyers, Montaigne mentions the "ingenious opinion" of Isocrates who advised the king "to make the trades and negotiations of his subjects free, gratuitous, and lucrative, and their disputes and quarrels onerous." Montaigne also points to a time in their own history when the French were not governed under Latin laws: "I am grateful to fortune that, so our historians say, it was a Gascon gentleman, and from my part of the country, who first opposed Charlemagne when he wanted to give us Latin and imperial laws." By specifying that this unnamed man was from his part of the country, Montaigne associates himself with this Gascon gentleman who opposed Charlemagne's innovation. In addition to the burdens forced on private life by the Latin laws, the result of their imposition is the barbarous but lawful custom of having to purchase justice and being denied justice if one cannot pay. Thus, Montaigne says, to the three ancient estates of Church, Nobility, and People, a fourth has been added, the estate of lawyers that has sovereign authority over life and property.

In *Montaigne's Politics: Authority and Governance in the Essais*, Biancamaria Fontana describes the legal situation to which Montaigne refers: "An unfortunate combination of Roman law and feudal custom had produced in France an aberrant result, a judicial monstrosity, which subsequent interventions on the part of the crown had only succeeded in making more incoherent and unmanageable.... France had far too many laws.... Moreover, many of these laws were obsolete or redundant, some contradicted one another, and all were expressed in a characteristically cryptic jargon." French law "was distinguished by its remarkable obscurity: people were governed by codes that were not even written in their own language, and that they could neither read nor understand without the costly assistance of specialists." This resulted in what Montaigne calls the barbarous custom of having to pay for justice. Fontana says that "Montaigne was strongly opposed to the venality that characterized the French judicial system. To begin with, he disapproved of the fact that magistrates generally expected to be remunerated for their services by the parties involved in trials: payments ranged from simple fees, in themselves rather modest, to far more substantial benefits, such as pensions, appointments, or gratuities."[6] In 1584, Montaigne drafted comments on a project of judicial reform intended for Henry of Navarre in which he expressed "his belief that there should be 'one single justice', and that consequently legal services should be free of charge and equally accessible to all, regardless of wealth and social position."[7]

Fontana's description explains the situation of the nobility that Montaigne finds monstrous as well as the existence of a

---

[6] Biancamaria Fontana, *Montaigne's Politics: Authority and Governance in the Essais* (Princeton: Princeton University Press, 2008) 27. See also R. Doucet, *Les Institutions de la France au xvi siècle*, 2 vols. (Paris: Éditions A. et J. Picard, 1948) especially vol 1. 60-61, where the distinction and the relationship between common or customary law and written Roman law are discussed. Doucet shows that the question of the laws was a vexed issue in the sixteenth century and that no province of the kingdom enjoyed unity of legislation. I am grateful to Professor William Beik for his help in uncovering Montaigne's meaning and for suggesting the Doucet volume to me.

[7] Fontana, *Montaigne's Politics*, 33. See also Philippe Desan, *Montaigne: Les formes du monde et de l'esprit* (Paris: Presses de l'Université Paris-Sorbonne, 2008) 176-77.

fourth estate, which was so oppressive to the poor. "In France the magistracy represented a powerful caste, a 'Fourth Estate'; yet in practice only the lowest ranks of the population were subjected to their authority and to the prescriptions of the law. The nobility followed a code of honor of its own, which often clashed with ordinary legislation and was deemed superior to it; among the members of the Third Estate, the rich could pay to secure a favorable treatment from judges and tribunals, so that only the poor were exposed to the full rigor of the law."[8] Montaigne says that "our French laws, by their irregularity and lack of form, rather lend a hand to the disorder and corruption that is seen in their administration and execution. Their commands are so confused and inconsistent that they are some excuse for both disobedience and faulty interpretation, administration, and observance" (III:13,821).

As Fontana shows, Montaigne was involved in contemporary efforts to reform the French judicial system; but his reform also goes much deeper. By pointing back to an ancient condition, a time before the imposition of burdensome Latin laws, Montaigne is suggesting change that is really a "restoration" of a condition within the history of the French people, a possibility that he discovers within that history. Through introducing the "ingenious opinion" of Isocrates, he points to the desirability of freeing the private sphere from the control of the laws as much as possible: the trade and negotiations of the people should be free, gratuitous, and

[8] Fontana, *Montaigne's Politics*, 28.

lucrative.[9] His restoration is not precisely a return to the past but the introduction of a new freedom.

The discussion of the barbarous situation of the nobility also points to a reform that is fundamental. In showing the contradictions between the laws of honor and the laws of justice, Montaigne refers to the dishonor incurred by enduring insult, specifically the insult of "being given the lie," that is, being accused of lying. Montaigne devotes an entire essay to this subject, "Du démentir" or "Of giving the lie." He begins by describing his own project in writing the *Essays*, how he has taken himself as the subject of his book. So the question arises of how we can believe that a man would actually tell the truth about himself. At this point, the discussion turns to the custom concerning the gravity of the insult of being given the lie: why do the French regard this as the extreme of insult? "Our nation," he says, "has long been reproached for this vice" of lying. Salvianus of Massilia, who lived at the time of the Emperor Valentinian, says that "to the French lying and perjury are not a vice but a manner of speaking." Montaigne goes further: "If a man wanted to go this testimony one better, he could say that [lying] is now a virtue to them. Men form and fashion themselves for it as for an honorable practice; for dissimulation is among the most notable qualities of this century" (II:18,505).

Given the French penchant for lying and also the honorable status of lying, Montaigne wonders "what could be the source of that custom, which we observe so religiously, of feeling more bitterly offended when reproached with this vice, which is so

---

[9] See Desan, *Montaigne: Les formes*, 171-73, for a very helpful discussion of the "new ethic" associated with the economic practices of the new merchant class which was developing in the 16th century.

common among us, than with any other; and that it should be the worst insult that can be given us in words, to reproach us with lying." One possible cause is that it is natural to defend oneself most for the defects of which we are most guilty. Perhaps we try to unburden ourselves of guilt by becoming resentful of the accusation. We condemn it in appearance although we have it in fact. Further, he makes the association between lying and cowardice: the reproach of lying is the accusation of cowardice and lack of courage. Indeed, there is no more obvious cowardice than to deny our own word and to deny what we know.

It is here that Montaigne sets out his understanding of the social bond and thus lays the new foundation of human association. Our word, he says, is the only instrument we have to communicate our thoughts and wills. "If it fails us, we have no more hold on each other, no more knowledge of each other. If it deceives us, it breaks up all our relations and dissolves all the bonds of society" (II:18,505). In "Of liars" he says, "Lying is an accursed vice. We are men, and hold together only by our word" (I:9,23).

Montaigne concludes "Of giving the lie" with the observation that, among the ancient Greeks and Romans, giving the lie was not considered so great an insult and did not result in violence and revenge. This indifference of the ancients looks "novel and strange" to us. So he wonders how it came to pass that giving the lie has become the extreme insult: "As for the varied etiquette of giving the lie, and our laws of honor in that matter, and the changes they have undergone, I shall put off to another time telling what I know about that, and shall meanwhile learn, if I can, at what time the custom began of weighing and measuring words so exactly, and attaching our honor to them" (II:18,506). In fact, he does not discuss this explicitly again in the *Essays*.

Montaigne's re-founding consists in his discovery, his invention, of truth as the foundation of society. He does this by taking the custom concerning giving the lie and directing it to its true end. This entails the reformation of the nobility through a transformed notion of honor and courage. That is why he so strongly associates lying with cowardice. He turns the desire for honor, expressed in revenge for the insult of giving the lie, into the notion of honor as keeping one's word, telling the truth, and communicating one's thoughts and will.

While most philosophers either hide under the authority of custom or reject custom entirely on account of the weakness of its origins, Montaigne discovers or invents the possibilities already present in the tradition. There are two senses of the possible that must be addressed with respect to Montaigne's invention. The first is the sense of the possible as that which is "realistic," what can reasonably be expected to be accomplished. This meaning amounts to a rejection of the notion of perfection as unrealizable in practice and therefore involves a concomitant lowering of expectations based on the idea that to aim at perfection is futile and dangerous. Perfection, the attainment of the highest and the best state of affairs, is really impossible.

The second sense of the possible is that of "what has never been seen before." According to this sense, the possible is distinguished both from the probable and from the actual. The fact that something has never existed in the past does not mean that it cannot ever exist, that it is impossible in principle. This is the openness to the possible that Montaigne has in mind when he says that his end is to tell not what has happened but what can happen (I:21,75).

Montaigne says that we must take men as we find them, already bound and formed to certain customs (III:9,730). This attitude toward the givenness of the human condition is what makes the difference between change and overthrowing everything, between re-founding and destroying. Both senses of the possible, then, are present here: the rejection of the hierarchical notion of perfection implied in his "taking men as we find them," and the introduction of a foundation of association that had never been seen before.

Michael Oakeshott describes this discovery of possibilities as the pursuit of "intimations." The amendment of traditional modes of behavior and of existing social arrangements is accomplished not by a process of making them conform to an ideology but "by exploring and pursuing what is intimated" in these traditional modes.[10] This is what preserves the continuity of a tradition: "authority is diffused between past, present and future; between the old, and new and what is to come."[11] This view of change and reform gives some assurance that "our mistakes of understanding will be less frequent and less disastrous."[12] As Biancamaria Fontana puts it, recovery must come "from the hidden resources of French society itself, from the community's potential for self-regeneration."[13]

---

[10] Michael Oakeshott, "Political Education," in *The Voice of Liberal Learning*, ed. Timothy Fuller (New Haven: Yale University Press, 1989; reprint, Indianapolis, IN: Liberty Fund, 2001) 173.

[11] Ibid., 179.

[12] Ibid., 175.

[13] Fontana, *Montaigne's Politics*, 114.

II. The Essay and the Social

Montaigne lived through the civil, religious wars of sixteenth-century France. Although he was a Catholic and remained loyal to the Catholic side, he was trusted by princes of both factions and was called upon to negotiate between them. He also reluctantly served two terms as Mayor of Bordeaux by virtue of the vote of the magistrates and at the insistence of the king. When he was thirty-nine years old, he retired from his judicial position in the parlement of Bordeaux to his family chateau and to his library where he found the solitude to allow his mind to entertain itself in idleness and freedom. But he soon found that the mind alone with itself generated and produced out of itself only "chimeras and fantastic monsters." He decided to put these in writing so that, in time, he might make his mind "ashamed of itself" (I:9,21). Thus the essay form was born, a new mode of philosophy that brings philosophy out of the isolated mind and makes it sociable.

David Hume, in his essay "Of essay-writing," argues that the essay form brings together what he calls the learned and the conversable worlds. "The separation of the learned from the conversable world," he says, "seems to have been the great defect of the last age, and must have had a very bad influence both on books and company." The social world suffers because, without the influence of philosophy, conversation is reduced to stories and gossip. But philosophy itself also suffers from this separation. Cut off from the world, philosophy becomes barbarous because it lacks "that liberty and facility of thought and expression which can only be acquired by conversation." Philosophy, Hume says, "went to wrack by this moaping recluse method of study, and became as chimerical in her conclusions as she was unintelligible in her stile and manner of delivery." Most important, philosophy suffers because experience, upon which philosophy rests, is to be found only "in common life and conversation." [14]

Thus, Pascal describes Montaigne's style as "totally composed of thoughts born out of the ordinary conversations of life."[15] As Erich Auerbach claims, Montaigne was the first author who wrote for the non-specialized but educated reader: "By the success of the *Essays* the educated public first revealed its existence."[16] That is, Montaigne actually discovers and brings this public into existence in the modern world. Michael Oakeshott sees the *Essays* as the clearest example of what he calls "the conversation of mankind." This conversation, he says, "is not only the greatest but also the most hardly sustained of all the accomplishments of mankind. Men have never been wanting who have had this understanding of human activity and intercourse, but few have embraced it without reserve and without misgiving, and on this account it is proper to mention the most notable of those who have done so: Michel de Montaigne."[17] That Montaigne embraced this activity "without reserve and without misgiving" is a manifestation of his generous sociability.

---

[14] David Hume, *Essays: Moral, Political, and Literary*, ed. Eugene F. Miller (Indianapolis: Liberty Classics, 1985) 534-35.

[15] Blaise Pascal, *Pensées et opuscules*, ed. Léon Brunschvicg, rev.ed. (Paris: Librairie Hachette, 1946) no. 18.

[16] Erich Auerbach, "L'humaine condition," in *Mimesis: The Representation of Reality in Western Literature*, trans. Willard R. Trask (Princeton: Princeton University Press, 1953) 308.

[17] Michael Oakeshott, *Rationalism in Politics and Other Essays*, ed. Timothy Fuller (London: Methuen, 1962; reprint, Indianapolis: Liberty Press, 1991) 491.

Montaigne makes his mind ashamed of itself by overcoming the conceit and the pride of the philosopher that he alone is most fully human on account of his superior intellect and that his mind, alone with itself, can determine the truth. As Hume says, philosophy, without the experience found in society, becomes "chimerical" in her conclusions. Whereas the mind alone with itself generates chimeras and fantastic monsters, the mind brought down into the social realm is grounded in the testimony and stories and opinions of other men. Reason is "essayed" or tested in the court of experience and is subjected to and corrected by experience. But this also means that the philosopher's mind is enlarged. The philosopher's prejudice that only what is familiar to him could be real and true is overcome in the openness to the possible that comes with trust in the testimony of others. The essay brings the philosopher down to his common humanity, to the human condition that he shares with all men. To paraphrase Hume: Montaigne is a philosopher but in the midst of all his philosophy, he is still a man.

The invention of society requires a radical transformation of philosophy itself. Philosophy must give up its claim to set the standard for what it means to be human, a standard which rests on the superior wisdom of the philosopher and which makes the philosopher divine. Montaigne describes himself as "a new figure: an unpremeditated and accidental philosopher" (II:12,409). When he is seized by the desire to tell his thoughts and his conduct, he calls on the help of ancient philosophy so that he might go out a bit more decently in public. He discovers to his astonishment that his thoughts and conduct conform by accident to many of the teachings and examples of ancient philosophy. In other words, his thoughts and conduct have not been formed by philosophy: he simply uses ancient philosophy to express publicly what he is. Unpremeditated and accidental philosophy is philosophy made social and it is the way in which the philosopher participates in society.

The invention of society also requires that the "great," i.e., those who claim the right to rule, become sociable. Just as the philosopher must be reminded that he is still a man, so also the prince must be brought down from his lofty throne to recognize his common humanity. "On the loftiest throne in the world we are still sitting on our own rump" (III:13,857). Montaigne actually begins the essay "Of the disadvantage of greatness" by mentioning what he takes to be the *advantage* of greatness: the great man can "step down" whenever he chooses (III:7,699). The disadvantage of greatness, on the other hand, is that it is very difficult for the sovereign to share in the most pleasant form of human association, the "essaying" or testing of oneself with other men. The prince can only test himself if he "steps down." Essaying can only occur in a condition in which the master gives up his conventional and customary power in order to depend upon only his natural abilities. In other words, the prince must be able to separate himself from his power, become a mere man just like every other man, in order to participate in society. Of his own role as mayor of Bordeaux, Montaigne says: "the Mayor and Montaigne have always been two, with a very clear separation." The judgment of the prince must be above his power. He must see his princely power as "an extraneous accident" and "know how to reveal himself" like any other man (III:10,774).

For Montaigne, society not only limits the power of the prince but also subordinates violence and force to the everyday life of the domestic and private. "When I see both Caesar and

Alexander, in the thick of their great tasks, so fully enjoying natural and therefore necessary and just pleasures, I do not say that that is relaxing their souls, I say that it is toughening them, subordinating these violent occupations and laborious thoughts, by the vigor of their spirits, to the practice of everyday life: wise men, had they believed that this [the violent] was their ordinary occupation, the other [the everyday] the extraordinary" (III:13,850). If the violent is what is really ordinary, then it would seem that the mastery and subjection of the weak by the strong is the ordinary or natural condition of man, and that political power is simply that mastery and subjection made legitimate. Montaigne's invention of society, then, is the overcoming and reversal of that condition: the good that is found in the social realm subjects the strong and violent to itself.

III. The Good of Society

The good of society is the enjoyment of the free association of men, freed from both the shame of the private and the domination of the political. In his discussion of "the totalitarian temptation," Roger Scruton describes a totalitarian government as "one that does not respect or acknowledge the distinction between civil society and State.... Under totalitarian rule society is itself a creation of the State, rather than the other way round."[18] Society serves as the limit on the power of government by preserving the intermediate sources of authority that the state has a tendency to try to crush. Montaigne insists on the independence and authority of the family and the Church. He sets out a vision of liberal education

---

[18] Roger Scruton, *A Political Philosophy* (London and New York: Continuum, 2006) 147.

that forms the character and the mind of the free individual, including the character that is necessary for friendship and for the free expression of opinion. Not only does society serve as the limit on political power, it is also the sphere in which the human good is found, where those activities that are "good in themselves" are pursued.

Marriage. Montaigne's views on marriage show clearly that he does not regard marriage as merely a matter of personal choice or as a contract entered into by two individuals. "We do not marry for ourselves, whatever we say; we marry just as much for our posterity, for our family. The practice and benefit of marriage concerns our family very far beyond us." Marriage "needs more solid and stable foundations" than sexual attraction or our own personal choices. (III:5,646). This view of marriage also means that he sees the family and society in general as a bond that transcends the here and now and includes the unborn. "We embrace both those who have been and those who are not yet" (III:746).

Economic freedom. Montaigne's insistence on the independence of the social from the political can be seen clearly in his stance toward economic freedom and the importance that economic freedom has for the authority of the family. As we have seen, Montaigne suggests the radical reform of the French legal system in "Of custom." The French, he says, are burdened with laws "which bind the people in all of their domestic affairs." He offers instead the "ingenious opinion" of Isocrates who advised his king "to make the trades and negotiations of his subjects free, gratuitous, and lucrative" (I:23,84-85).

C.S. Lewis takes Montaigne as his example of "the freeborn mind:" "In adult life it is the man who needs, and asks, nothing of government who can criticize its acts and snap his fingers at its ideology. Read Montaigne; that's the voice of a man with his legs under his own table, eating the mutton and turnips raised on his own land. Who will talk like that when the State is everyone's schoolmaster and employer?"[19] Lewis is here especially concerned with the role of economic independence in providing an education for one's children that is not controlled by the state.

Liberal education. In "Of the education of children" Montaigne says that the entire purpose of education is the formation of the judgment of the pupil especially through the study of history and philosophy. Like Montaigne's own education, the education he proposes would teach the pupil to be "wholly incapable of submitting to force and violence." Montaigne's friend, Etienne La Boétie, wrote a work on politics, *Voluntary Servitude*, that addresses this relationship between education and freedom. He argues that even among peoples who are subjected to tyranny, there are always some men who despise and want to shake off the yoke of servitude. That is why tyrants, who are aware "that books and learning more than anything else give men the sense and understanding to know one another and to hate tyranny," want no learned men among their subjects.[20] Liberal education is not for the purpose of producing good subjects for the regime, but free men of independent judgment.

---

[19] C. S. Lewis, *God in the Dock: Essays on Theology and Ethics*. ed. Walter Hooper (Grand Rapids, Mich.: William B. Eerdmans, 1970) 314.

[20] Etienne de La Boétie, *Le discours de la servitude volontaire*, texte etabli par P. Léonard (Paris: Payot, 1985) 134-35. I have relied upon David Lewis Schaefer's translation of the *Discourse* in *Freedom over Servitude*, ed. David Lewis Schaefer (Westport, CT: Greenwood Press, 1998) 205.

The education that Montaigne recommends includes the study of history so that the young man might form his independent judgment. The histories teach us to know men in their individuality. Men who love freedom must be able to recognize each other. La Boétie says that the mutual recognition of freedom-loving men is made almost impossible under the tyrant because freedom of speech is prohibited.[21]

Freedom of speech. A character of a certain kind is required for the practice of freedom of speech and Montaigne's character comes through especially clearly in his description of himself with respect to this practice. He does not at all hate opinions contrary to his own. He enters into discussion and argument with great freedom and ease: "No propositions astonish me, no belief offends me, whatever contrast it offers with my own.... When someone opposes me, he arouses my attention, not my anger" (III:8,705). Montaigne associates the inability to converse in this manner with a tyrannical disposition: "it is always a tyrannical ill humor to be unable to endure a way of thinking different from your own" (III:8,709). In fact, in what may be the only instance in the *Essays* where he refers to himself as perfect, he says with respect to bantering and joking: "I am perfect in forbearance, for I endure retaliation, not only sharp but even indiscreet, without being disturbed" (III:8,717).

Truth is the social bond that is possible for free individuals: free speech is the way in which diverse minds can be bound to each other. Society is brought about through self-communication. The only way we can know each other is

---

[21] Ibid., 135 (Schaefer, *Freedom over Servitude,* 206).

through our words in which we communicate our thoughts and wills, i.e., our judgments.

Friendship. Montaigne is one of the few modern political philosophers who regard friendship as a philosophical topic. Hobbes and Rousseau, for example, are primarily concerned with preventing the development of factions. But Montaigne sees friendship as a greater good than citizenship. In "Of friendship" many of the friendships of antiquity are presented as examples of opposition to tyranny. Describing the friendship of Caius Blossius and Tiberius Gracchus, who were condemned for conspiracy by the Roman consuls, Montaigne says that "they were friends more than citizens, friends [to each other] more than friends or enemies of their country." As Montaigne's friend La Boétie reminds us, tyrants have no friends and cannot tolerate the friendships of their subjects because they are always suspicious of conspiracies. La Boétie argues that friendship requires a character that is not motivated by fear. Friendship only occurs between honorable people, for it arises only from mutual esteem. "What renders a friend assured of the other is the knowledge of his integrity."[22]

Religion. The question of Montaigne's sincerity with respect to religious belief has always been a source of deep disagreement among his readers. Here, I put aside the issues of his sincerity and orthodoxy and focus on the role that religion—and the Catholic Church in particular—plays in his political philosophy. Although Montaigne opposes the Reformation on both metaphysical and political grounds, he also opposes the use of violence in matters of conscience, including the execution of heretics. His essay "Of freedom of

[22] Ibid., 160 (Schaefer, *Freedom over Servitude*, 220).

conscience" suggests that he acknowledges that the religious wars of his day placed severe limits on what was possible in matters of religious unity. In the end, it seems he bowed to necessity and accepted the practice of religious toleration, but he held that division of religion weakened the social bond.

Montaigne is, I believe, the only early modern political philosopher who defends the Catholic Church in its universality, the only one who does not recommend that it be subordinated to the state, or that it merely be tolerated as one among many religions within the state. The Church transcends the limits of the political and stands as an independent authority and, therefore, as a limit on the power of the state.

Montaigne's father had sent him to the poorest village in his neighborhood to be nursed and had him held over the baptismal font by villagers of the lowest condition in order to attach him and oblige him to them (III:13,844). For Montaigne, the spiritual power of the Church is inextricably linked to the transformation of the relation between the nobility and the people. It is, after all, his baptism that unites him to the poorest of the poor. Eamon Duffy insists on "the social homogeneity of late medieval religion."[23] As he demonstrates, "rich and poor, simple and sophisticate could kneel side by side, using the same prayers and sharing the same hopes." In spite of the differences of sophistication about the faith "they did not have a different religion."[24]

In his essay, "The Nature and Meaning of Sociality," Oakeshott argues that "God is the only principle of sociability

[23] Eamon Duffy, *The Stripping of the Altars: Traditional Religion in England 1400-1580* (New Haven and London: Yale University Press 1992) 265.

[24] Ibid., 298.

which will explain the facts of life. Society becomes possible [only] by religion." Thus, Oakeshott interprets "God is Love" to mean "God is the only principle of sociality."[25]

The Church offers the possibility of union among men that transcends natural and social inequality and is based on a foundation of truth. The foundation of Montaigne's new form of society is truth. Not only does Christianity claim to be true, it holds that truth to be accessible to all men, to the most simple peasant woman as to the most learned theologian. Thus, the pride of the philosopher (that he is among the few who possess the truth) is overcome in the submission of the philosopher to the "old ways" of the simple (II:54,227).

The Church is "that great common way" (II:12,387). The distinction between the learned and the common herd does not obtain within the Church, for there "we are all the vulgar" (II:12,429). As Roger Scruton observes: "When religious faith declines it becomes difficult for intellectuals to believe that they really belong to the same community as ordinary people."[26]

Montaigne considers all men his compatriots. "I embrace a Pole as I do a Frenchman, setting this national bond after the universal and common one" (III:9,743). The universal and common bond has its source in a universal and common city. Rome is "the only common and universal city. The sovereign magistrate who commands there is acknowledged equally elsewhere. It is the metropolitan city of all Christian nations; the Spaniard and the Frenchman, every man is at home there. To be one of the princes of that state one need only be of Christendom, wherever it may be" (III:9,763). In his *Travel*

---

[25] Michael Oakeshott, *Religion, Politics and the Moral Life*, ed. Timothy Fuller (New Haven: Yale University Press, 1993) 59-60.

[26] Scruton, *A Political Philosophy*, 112.

Journal, Montaigne makes a similar claim: Rome is "the most universal city in the world, a place where strangeness and differences of nationality are considered least; for by its nature it is a city pieced together out of foreigners; everyone is as if at home. Its ruler embraces Christendom with his authority; his princely jurisdiction is binding on foreigners in their own homes just as here. At his own election and that of all the princes and grandees of his court the consideration of their origin has no weight."[27] The Church is the society in which the origins do not matter. It offers the only possibility for multi-cultural society.

In his "Notes towards the Definition of Culture," T.S. Eliot describes the conditions for the kind of common culture that Montaigne presupposes: "While we believe that the same religion may inform a variety of cultures, we may ask whether any culture could come into being, or maintain itself, without a religious basis. We may go further and ask whether what we call the culture, and what we call the religion, of a people are not different aspects of the same thing: the culture being, essentially, the incarnation (so to speak) of the religion of a people."[28] The situation Eliot describes is one in which "the culture of an artist or a philosopher is distinct from that of a mine worker or a field labourer; the culture of a poet will be

---

[27] Montaigne, *Œuvres complètes*, ed. Albert Thibaudet and Maurice Rat (Paris: Gallimard, 1962) 1236 (F961). References to the English translation of the *Travel Journal* are to *The Complete Works of Montaigne*, trans. Donald M. Frame (Stanford, CA.: Stanford University Press, 1943).

[28] T. S. Eliot, *Christianity and Culture: The Idea of a Christian Society and Notes towards the Definition of Culture* (New York: Harcourt, Brace and World, 1949) 101.

somewhat different from that of a politician; but in a healthy society these are all parts of the same culture."[29]

IV. The Character of the Free Individual

Society is the realm of freedom, where diverse human beings can pursue the good, each in his own way, in peace. It takes a character that is both free and sociable to make a free society possible, and that character can only be formed by and within the intermediate institutions that the state seeks to crush.

The freedom of this character might be described as the condition of being "neither master nor slave," the character that does not seek to dominate others but, at the same time, will not submit to force. Rousseau says in the *Discourse on the Origin and Foundation of Inequality*: "It is very difficult to reduce to obedience one who does not seek command."[30] In order to be free, in order not to be a slave, one must first renounce the desire to be a master. Montaigne's love of freedom expresses itself in his hatred of "every sort of tyranny, both in words and acts." When he says: "I am disgusted with mastery both active and passive," he explains what he means through the example of Otanes, who had the right to pretend to the throne of Persia but who abandoned that right to his companions provided that he and his family be allowed to live in the empire "outside of all subjection and mastery" except that of the ancient laws. Otanes could not support either commanding or being commanded. Montaigne says that

[29] Ibid.,198.

[30] Jean-Jacques Rousseau, *Discourse on the Origin and Foundation of Inequality*, in *The First and Second Discourses*, trans. Roger D. and Judith R. Masters (New York: St. Martin's Press, 1964) 173.

Otanes took the course of action that he himself would willingly have taken (III:7,700).

The man who is neither master nor slave, then, must also be courageous, willing to fight for his freedom. Courage requires what the Greeks called *thumos* or spiritedness. As Harvey Mansfield shows in his discussion of "manliness," modern political philosophy seeks to curb spiritedness severely because it sees it as the greatest threat to political stability and peace: the spirited man cannot be controlled as easily as the fearful, servile type.[31] Montaigne is an exception to this tendency. He is willing to die for his country—indeed he fought in the civil wars and risked all he had for his king—but he does not seek his own good in his public role. His hatred of tyranny expresses itself especially in his open speaking, whether to the princes for whom he negotiates, in his conversation, or in the *Essays*.

The invention of society, then, entails bringing into existence a new moral character consisting especially of two new virtues, i.e., integrity and generosity. The meaning of integrity is captured in Montaigne's description of himself as "neither master nor slave." The invention of society is based on generosity, the virtue that replaces the classical virtue of magnanimity or greatness of soul. Montaigne says: "If my heart is not great enough, it is compensatingly open" (III:7,700). Generosity is the openness of heart that reveals and communicates itself to others and invites a similar response from others. That is precisely what the *Essays* do.

The free and generous individual possesses and enjoys the good that is society. In "Of experience" Montaigne writes: "In my opinion, from the most ordinary, common, and familiar

---

[31] Harvey Mansfield, *Manliness* (New Haven and London: Yale University Press, 2006) chapter 6.

things, if we could put them in their proper light, can be formed the greatest miracles of nature and the most marvelous examples, especially on the subject of human actions" (III:13,829). The most common human actions, seen in their proper light, are not shameful and servile, but social. Everyday life is miraculous because it subjects the violent impulses to itself. The *Essays* of Montaigne are the revelation of the miracle of ordinary life.

2

Belonging to Oneself: Montaigne on Moral Autonomy

Christopher Edelman

In the essay "Of repentance," Montaigne proclaims his moral autonomy, explaining to readers that he lives according to his own laws and that he judges himself in his own court. Montaigne does not explicitly elaborate on this claim to govern himself, and thus he leaves us—as he so often does—in the position of having to use his *Essais* to rationally reconstruct what exactly he might mean. It seems to me that such a reconstruction is well worth our while, since on this issue—as on so many others—Montaigne has something unique to say. [1] My aim in this essay, then, is to offer an account of Montaigne's understanding of autonomy, one which I hope will allow us to appreciate more fully the contribution that Montaigne has to make to our own understanding of what it might mean to achieve some degree of self-governance.

---

[1] Montaigne's conception of moral autonomy has not received a great deal of attention from historians of philosophy. One exception, however, is J.B. Schneewind. See his monograph, *The Invention of Autonomy* (Cambridge: Cambridge University Press, 1998) and his essay, "Montaigne on Moral Philosophy and the Good Life," in *The Cambridge Companion to Montaigne* (Cambridge: Cambridge University Press, 2005) especially 224.

I

It is likely the case that when contemporary philosophers hear the term "autonomy" they immediately think of Kant, and this is not without reason. But of course the notion of autonomy or self-governance pre-dates Kant. We might begin with Plato. In the *Republic*, Plato portrays self-governance as analogous to the governance of the *polis*. In the same way that justice in the *polis* is defined by each member of the community "doing his own work," so justice in the soul is defined by the parts of the soul doing their own work, all under the guidance of the reasoning part:

> But in truth justice was, as it seems, something of this sort; however, not with respect to a man's minding his external business, but with respect to what is within, with respect to what truly concerns him and his own. He doesn't let each part in him mind other people's business or the three classes in the soul meddle with each other, but really sets his own house in good order and rules himself (*arxanta auton*); he arranges himself, becomes his own friend, and harmonizes the three parts, exactly like three notes in a harmonic scale, lowest, highest, and middle. And if there are some other parts in between, he binds them together and becomes entirely one from many, moderate and harmonized.[2]

This way of characterizing self-rule is of course in part a product of the fact that Socrates, Glaucon, and Adeimantus have chosen to treat the city and the soul as analogously structured. And yet the notion of self-rule as a sort of self-mastery that is achieved when reason governs the passions is

---

[2] Plato, *The Republic of Plato*, trans. Allan Bloom (New York: Basic Books, 1991) 123 (443d).

not uncharacteristic of ancient Greek and Roman conceptions of self-rule in general. It is also characteristic of ancient Greek and Roman conceptions of self-rule that the rule of reason over the passions is taken to be internally related to moral virtue.

Montaigne himself recognizes this, and holds out Socrates and Cato as moral exemplars in this regard. In "Of cruelty" he remarks their success at using reason to habituate their souls to virtue to such an extent that it became second nature to them. Montaigne tells us that they represent the highest degree of virtue, followed by those who, unable to form their souls so decisively, must continue to do battle with their passions. Finally, the third rank of virtuous men includes those who have an inborn distaste for debauchery and vice. Montaigne is not even sure whether to refer to this last class of men as virtuous, and he counts himself among them:

> "I am so far from having arrived at that first and most perfect degree of excellence where virtue becomes a habit, that even of the second degree I can hardly give any proof. I have not put myself to great effort to curb the desires by which I have found myself pressed. My virtue is a virtue, or should I say an innocence, that is accidental and fortuitous... Thus I cannot give myself any great thanks because I find myself free from many vices... I owe it more to my fortune than my reason" (II:11.311). [3]

Montaigne in fact goes to great lengths to point out that he does not now and has not in the past aimed to conquer his passions through the use of reason. For example, one of the

---

[3] All translations come from *The Complete Essays of Montaigne*, trans. Donald Frame (Stanford: Stanford UP 1958). Parenthetical citations to Montaigne's text contain the book, chapter, and page number of Frame's translation).

major themes in the essay "Of repentance" is the effect that aging has on the body and its desires. These days, Montaigne says, his reason may get the better of his passions, but that is only because his passions have been diminished by old age. Unlike Cephalus in book one of the *Republic*, Montaigne expresses no gratitude for the fact that growing old has diminished his libido, and he is not proud of his chaste behavior as an old man. Moreover, he writes that in his more licentious days he full well recognized "the face of vice in voluptuousness" (III:2,619) and he does not repent for the fact that in his youth his lust often got the better of his reason. He knew what he was doing, and he recognized its sinfulness, and yet he did not attempt to reform. This lack of interest in the project of self-discipline for the sake of self-mastery is confirmed in "Of physiognomy," where he writes: "I have not, like Socrates, corrected my natural disposition by force of reason, and have not troubled my inclination at all by art. I let myself go as I have come. I combat nothing" (III:12,811).

II

It is not simply that Montaigne is not interested in pursuing Platonic self-mastery. For in addition to his lack of interest in self-mastery, Montaigne calls into question the moral authority of reason, and in doing so, he presents us with an alternative not only to the Platonic conception of moral autonomy with which he is familiar, but also to the Kantian conception which was yet to come. For the Platonic and Kantian conceptions seem to agree on at least this much: that autonomy essentially has to do with the rule of practical reason over the passions. Thus Kant's distinction between autonomy and heteronomy is a distinction between judgments based on reason versus judgments based on inclination. Montaigne, on the other hand, doubts the ability of what is variously referred to as "reason" or the "reasoning part of the soul" to serve as an objective guide to the good: "I always call reason (*raison*) that semblance of intellect that each man fabricates in himself. That reason, of which, by its condition, there can be a hundred different contradictory ones about one and the same subject, is an instrument of lead and of wax, stretchable, pliable, and adaptable to all biases and measures; all that is needed is the ability to mold it" (II:12,425).

Moreover, Montaigne's conception of autonomy diverges from Kant's in another respect. Whereas Kant goes so far as to identify autonomy and freedom of the will, Montaigne seems deliberately to problematize both the notion of free will and certain theoretical notions of moral responsibility that are often thought to go with it. Returning to "Of repentance," for example, we find Montaigne highlighting the problem of moral responsibility from the very beginning. Hence the opening lines of the essay: "Others form man; I tell of him, and portray a particular one, very ill-formed, whom I should really make very different from what he is if I had to fashion him over again (*de nouveaux*)" (III:2,610). Here Montaigne seems to suggest that he has fashioned himself, and so that he is responsible for how he has turned out. Then, later on in the essay, Montaigne offers what seems to be a deliberately hyperbolic account of his moral responsibility: "My judgment takes all the blame or all the praise for [my actions]; and the blame it takes, it always keeps, for virtually since its birth it has been one; the same inclination, the same road, the same strength. And in the matter of general opinions, in childhood I established myself (*je me logeay*) in the position where I was to remain" (III:2,616). For a thinker so sensitive to the powers of custom, this is a truly astonishing remark. Indeed, it is made all the more astonishing one page later, when he goes from one extreme to the other, apparently disavowing both freedom and ultimate responsibility for his actions: "As for me, I may desire in a general way to be different; I may condemn and dislike my nature as a whole, and implore God to reform me completely and to pardon my natural weakness. But this I ought not to call repentance, it seems to me, any more than my displeasure at being neither an angel nor Cato. My actions are in order and conformity with what I am and with my condition. I can do no better. And repentance does not properly apply to things that are not in our power; rather does regret" (III:2,617).

Juxtaposed as they are in "Of repentance," these hyperbolic accounts of freedom and responsibility on the one hand, and the lack thereof on the other hand, problematize our commonsensical notions of free will and moral responsibility. In doing so, they are consistent with Montaigne's approach to the issues of free will and responsibility elsewhere in the *Essais*. In the "Apology for Raymond Sebond," for example, he suggests that based on the principle of analogy, we have no more reason for believing our wills to be free than we do for believing that animals' wills are free (II:12,336). And later on in that same essay, he reflects on the possibility that all things, including human beliefs, judgments, and opinions are governed by nature (II:12,433). While there is not space here for a fully developed discussion of Montaigne's understanding of free will and moral responsibility, it is safe to say that Montaigne's understanding of the moral autonomy he claims to possess in

"Of repentance" is not founded upon any theoretical assertion of the existence of free will.

III

While Montaigne's account of autonomy differs from Kant's in at least these two fundamental ways, it is consistent with Kant's account insofar as it locates moral autonomy in the autonomy of one's judgment. That Montaigne locates moral autonomy in the autonomy of his judgment becomes evident in "Of repentance" when he discusses the problem of accurately identifying vices. On the one hand, it seems that we can trust our own conscience: "There is no vice truly a vice which is not offensive, and which a sound judgment does not condemn" (III:2,612). Yet on the other hand, he notes that perhaps this principle fails to take into account "the sin that is in the robes of state, that dwells in us as in its own home" (III:2,613). Either way, however, he does not place his trust in the judgment of others. Instead, he insists that one must cling to one's own judgment: "I have my own laws and court to judge me, and I address myself to them more than anywhere else" (III:2,613).[4]

The question, then, is what—according to Montaigne—makes his judgment, or his laws, or his court, specifically *his own*. This question is complicated for Montaigne due to his sensitivity to the formative powers of custom, for throughout the *Essais* he draws our attention to the ways that custom seems

---

[4]"*Nous autre principalement, qui vivons une vie privée qui n'est en montre qu'à nous, devons avoir estably un patron au dedans, auquel toucher nos actions, et, selon iceluy, nous caresser tantost, tantost nous chastier. J'ay mes loix et ma court pour juger de moy, et m'y adresse plus qu'ailleurs*" (VS 807).

to govern our judgment: "The principal effect of the power of custom is to seize and ensnare us in such a way that it is hardly within our power to get ourselves back out of its grip and return into ourselves to reflect and reason about its ordinances. In truth, because we drink them with our milk from birth, and because the face of the world presents itself in this aspect to our first view, it seems we are born on condition of following this course. And the common notions that we find in credit around us and infused into our soul by our fathers' seed, these seem to be the universal and natural ones" (I:23,83). This is not to say, however, that Montaigne thinks that achieving autonomy is a matter of casting off customary judgments in favor of what is natural or innate. For in the first place, he is skeptical of our ability to peel off the layers of custom in order to discover our underlying nature (see III:13.827 and III:10,772). But perhaps more importantly, judgments that he suspects of being natural or innate are not for all that judgments he wishes to call his own. In "Of the resemblance of children to fathers" he writes that "all those predispositions that are born in us without reason are bad; they are a kind of disease that we must combat" (II:37,580).

For Montaigne, then, the distinction between autonomous and heteronomous judgments does not map onto the distinction between judgments that are customary and those that are natural or innate. Both customary and natural judgments can be autonomous. This seems to come out in his essay "Of the education of children," where he writes: "Truth and reason are common to everyone, and no more belong to the man who first spoke them than to the man who says them later. It is no more according to Plato than according to me, since he and I understand and see it in the same way. The bees plunder the flowers here and there, but afterward they make of them honey, which is all theirs; it is no longer thyme or marjoram. Even so with pieces borrowed from others; [our student] will transform and blend them to make *a work that is all his own, to wit, his judgment.* His education, work, and study aim only at forming this" (I:26,111, my emphasis). Here Montaigne emphasizes the autonomy of judgment as the aim of the education of children. But clearly the program for the cultivation of students' judgment that he lays out in this chapter is virtually identical with one of the fundamental projects of his *Essais.*[5]

Thus in "Of the education of children" Montaigne prescribes that "the tutor make his charge pass everything through a sieve and lodge nothing in his head on mere authority and trust... For if he embraces Xenophon's and Plato's opinions by his own reasoning, they will no longer be theirs, they will be his. He who follows another follows nothing" (I:26,111). Passing everything through the sieve of one's judgment seems an apt expression for his own practice of essaying his judgment, which Montaigne describes in "Of Democritus and Heraclitus":

> Judgment is a tool to use on all subjects, and comes in everywhere. Therefore in the tests (*essais*) that I make of it here, I use every sort of occasion. If it is a subject I do not understand at all, even on that I essay my judgment, sounding the ford from a good distance; and then, finding it too deep for my height, I stick to the bank. And this acknowledgment

---

[5] Raymond La Charité, *The Concept of Judgment in Montaigne* (The Hague: Martinus Nijhoff, 1968) writes: "'*De l'institution des enfans*' is not only a pedagogical program; it is also Montaigne's own personal creation, the system by which he has developed and strengthened his own '*jugment naturel*' (p. 15).

> that I cannot cross over is a token of its action, indeed one of those it is most proud of. Sometimes in a vain and nonexistent subject I try (*j'essaye*) to see if it will find the wherewithal to give it body, prop it up, and support it. Sometimes I lead it to a noble and well-worn subject in which it has nothing original to discover, the road being so beaten that it can only walk in others' footsteps. There it plays its part by choosing the way that seems best to it, and of a thousand paths it says that this one or that was the most wisely chosen. (I:50,219)

For instance, in "Of cruelty," Montaigne essays, or tests, what he takes to be his natural antipathy toward cruelty. He is not sure whether his hatred of cruelty is innate, or whether it was infused in him by his upbringing, but there is no doubt that this aversion to cruelty is firmly entrenched in his soul. In the essay, then, he discusses his hatred of cruelty, and then goes on to adduce reasons for condemning cruelty by considering it from a number of different points of view. As a Christian, he condemns it because he argues that Christians, who "ought to have some concern about sending souls away in a good state," ought not to make dying souls desperate and agitated by unbearable tortures. As a fellow human being, he sympathetically reflects on torture from the perspective of the tortured, and as a citizen, he argues that torture serves no political purpose. It is because he has essayed his opinion of cruelty, then, that he can say that "Among other vices, I cruelly hate cruelty, both by nature *and by judgment*, as the extreme of all vices" (II:11,313 my emphasis). Thus, by essaying his opinion of cruelty, he transforms a pre-reflective opinion into a judgment that is more fully his own, insofar as it is now a judgment that he has reflectively endorsed. In other words, by reflexively judging his judgments, he engages in the act of self-appropriation.

While Montaigne sometimes affirms his pre-reflective opinions, in other cases he rejects them. For example, in "It is folly to measure the true and the false by our own capacity," Montaigne begins with the fact that "we attribute facility in belief and conviction to simplicity and ignorance" (I:27,132). He argues that this is not without reason, and yet it is also confused if it leads us to disdain and condemn as false whatever does not seem likely to us. He used to do this himself, he tells us, but upon reflection he has concluded that this was presumptuous on his part, and that "we must judge with more reverence the infinite power of nature, and with more consciousness of our ignorance and weakness" (II:27,133). Montaigne does not say that the customary judgment regarding the relation of credulousness to ignorance is simply wrong, nor that his conclusion concerning his presumption has changed his judgments regarding these reports of returning spirits, prognostications, and sorcery. In fact, he tells us explicitly that he still judges these reports to be false. But of course he has transformed his understanding of those judgments that he makes regarding the truth-value of these reports, thereby transforming the judgments themselves. While he judges that the reports are false, it is not because he thinks he knows that the events they relate are impossible. Thus, by judging his judgments concerning reports of extraordinary occurrences, Montaigne takes reflective ownership over his incredulousness while rejecting his former judgment concerning the impossibility of such events.

In these examples, then, we see Montaigne testing opinions by passing them through the sieve of his judgment. In doing so, he either makes them more fully his own, or he abandons them. In reflectively endorsing some of these opinions, Montaigne actively transforms them into reflective judgments, insofar as he provides them with a new foundation, namely his own understanding. In this sense, essaying himself is a method of taking control of himself, in that he achieves a greater degree of authorship over these opinions than he had prior to essaying them. This is of course not to say that these judgments that he retains are true or "rational," or that they ultimately originate in Montaigne's natural character, or that they issue from Montaigne's free will. But it is to say that they are more his own than other judgments that he has not similarly tested. It is this self-appropriation that he views as the essence of moral autonomy, and which is part and parcel of his general desire for moral and political independence: "The greatest thing in the world is to know how to belong to oneself" (I:39,178).

IV

At this point we might begin to wonder whether those commentators who have linked Montaigne with Richard Rorty have been on to something.[6] For I have been suggesting that

[6] David Hiley, in "The Politics of Skepticism: Reading Montaigne." *History of Philosophy Quarterly* 9, no. 4 (1992): 379-399, argues that Montaigne and Rorty share the desire for "a form of private irony and public responsibility" and that Montaigne provides us with a more compelling account of the private side of the ironic life (p. 380). Jack Abecassis, in "'Le Maire et Montaigne ont tousjours este deux, d'une separation bien claire': Public Necessity and Private Freedom in Montaigne," *MLN* 110, no. 5 (1995): 1067-1089) writes: "Montaigne's essayistic practice satisfies all the Rortian conditions for irony and… ultimately this irony provides the theoretical basis for his strict separation of

one of Montaigne's fundamental goals in his *Essais* is the achievement of a greater degree of moral autonomy, and that this autonomy is to be understood in terms of self-appropriation. And of course the fundamental goal of Rorty's liberal ironist—as detailed in *Contingency, Irony, and Solidarity*—is also autonomy, which Rorty seems to understand as essentially a matter of self-appropriation. The ironist, Rorty writes, "is trying… to get out from under an old final vocabulary and fashion one which will be all his own." In other words, "He wants to be able to sum up his life in his own terms. The perfect life will be one which closes in the assurance that the last of his final vocabularies, at least, really was wholly *his*."[7]

Indeed, there are a number of points of contact between Montaigne's and Rorty's conceptions of autonomy and selfhood. Neither views autonomy as grounded upon the freedom of the will, and both draw our attention to the sense in which the self is contingent. Thus Rorty uses Freud to depict moral consciousness as historically conditioned, idiosyncratic, and "as much a product of time and chance as political or

---

the private from the public, that is, the separation of the exercise of reason from political practice" (p. 1071). See also Alven Neiman, "Ironic Schooling: Socrates, Pragmatism and the Higher Learning," *Educational Theory* 41, no. 4 (1991): 371-384. Ann Hartle, on the other hand, has tried to place some distance between Montaigne and Rorty. See Ann Hartle, "Autonomy and Cruelty: Rorty and Montaigne on the Social Bond," in *Democracy Reconsidered*, ed. Elizabeth Kaufer Busch and Peter Augustine Lawler (New York: Lexington Books, 2009) 67-77. Hartle argues that whereas autonomy for Rorty is achieved through a self-creating act that isolates one from his community, autonomy for Montaigne is achieved through engaging, rather than casting off, the traditions of his community.

[7] Richard Rorty, *Contingency, Irony, and Solidarity* (Cambridge: Cambridge University Press, 1991) 97.

aesthetic consciousness,"[8] while Montaigne remarks how many of the basic terms of his final vocabulary, to use Rorty's language, appear to be contingent upon custom: "Another region, other witnesses, similar promises and threats, might imprint upon us in the same way a contrary belief. We are Christians by the same title that we are Perigordians" (II:12,325). Whereas Rorty speaks in terms of the contingency of one's conscience, Montaigne refers to the role that "Fortune" has played in providing him with his idiosyncratic moral dispositions: "My virtue is a virtue, or should I say an innocence, that is accidental and fortuitous. If I had been born with a more unruly disposition, I fear it would have gone pitifully with me" (II:11,311).

Moreover, both see the self as multifarious. Again, Rorty uses Freud, to "substitute a tissue of contingent relations, a web which stretches backward and forward through past and future time, for a formed, unified, present, self-contained substance, something capable of being seen steadily and whole."[9] Meanwhile, Montaigne claims that in portraying himself he portrays passing rather than being (III:2,611), and writes: "We are all patchwork, and so shapeless and diverse in composition that each bit, each moment, plays its own game. And there is as much difference between us and ourselves as there is between us and others" (II:1,244). This multifariousness is evident even in our convictions: "we are, I know not how, double within ourselves, with the result that we do not believe what we

---

[8] Rorty, *Contingency,* 30.

[9] Rorty, *Contingency,* 41. See also p. 33: "Freud thus helps us take seriously the possibility that there is no central faculty, no central self, called 'reason'—and thus to take Nietzschean pragmatism and perspectivalism seriously."

believe, and we cannot rid ourselves of what we condemn" (II:16,469).

This is why Montaigne will go along with Rorty in rejecting any identification of the self with reason or the rational part of the soul. To make such an identification involves one in a subtle dissociation of oneself from certain types of behavior, desires, feelings, or thoughts that in the end, Montaigne and Rorty would argue, do most certainly belong to oneself. Hence Montaigne's distrust of repentance, which seems to strike him as an opportunity for self-deception, insofar as it can aid us in disavowing our own will and identifying ourselves with what is truly only one part of our being while dissociating ourselves with another equally real part of ourselves. As usual, for both moral and intellectual reasons, Montaigne insists that we do not privilege one part of the human being at the expense of the others.[10]

Finally, both Rorty and Montaigne recognize the ambiguities that lie at the heart of the pursuit of autonomy. For on the one hand, Montaigne's project of essaying himself can be described in terms of self-constitution or self-transformation, insofar as by deliberately essaying himself, he alters—in one way or another—the beliefs, attitudes, and values that in large part constitute his very being. On the other hand, it also seems appropriate to describe his self-essaying in terms of self-representation or self-discovery, insofar as he clearly takes himself to be engaged in a project of self-study. Moreover, these two descriptions of his pursuit of autonomy seem to demand qualification by reference to the other. For instance,

---

[10] On Montaigne's refusal to deny any of his parts or actions as properly his own, see Telma de Souza Birchal, "Montaigne impenitent: la question du moi dans 'Du repentir' ", *Montaigne Studies*, vol. 23 (2011): 205-224.

to talk simply of self-transformation and the achievement of self-governance suggests too robust a conception of his own agency in the process of essaying himself. It implies the idea of the Cartesian subject, who exerts complete control over his judgment, insofar as his judgment is a product of his will. And yet to talk simply of self-description and self-discovery suggests too weak a conception of agency, as though Montaigne were not responsible for the judgments that he makes.

Montaigne recognizes, then, an ineliminable ambiguity in his act of essaying himself, such that any unqualified account of his relation to the self that he essays—whether in terms of self-constitution or self-discovery—is necessarily inadequate.[11] Hence somewhat paradoxical passages such as the following:

> In modeling this figure upon myself, I have had to fashion and compose myself so often to bring myself out, that the model itself has to some extent grown firm and taken shape. Painting myself for others, I have painted my inward self with colors clearer than my original ones. I have no more made my book than my book has made me—a book consubstantial with its author, concerned with my own self, an integral part of my life; not concerned with some third-hand, extraneous purpose, like all other books. Have I wasted my time by taking stock of myself so continually, so carefully? For those who go over themselves only in their minds and occasionally in speech do not penetrate the essentials of their examination as does a man who makes that his study, his work, and his trade, who binds himself to keep an enduring account, with all his faith, with all his strength. (II:18,504)

[11] For an insightful and detailed discussion of the ambiguity involved in Montaigne's act of self-appropriation, see Jean Starobinski, *Montaigne in Motion*, trans. Arthur Goldhammer (Chicago: University of Chicago Press, 1985), pp. 217-222. Thanks to Daniel Cullen for pointing this out to me.

Here Montaigne begins by suggesting that in making his book, he is making his very self, and this is no doubt true, insofar as by essaying himself, he is actively constituting himself, altering the course of what he is and will be. And yet, to simply talk of self-constitution here fails to acknowledge the sense in which essaying is, again, an activity of discovering the self that is already there, albeit implicitly. Hence the final lines in this passage about "taking stock" and "penetrating the essentials" of the examination, lines that without the earlier language of self-constitution, would themselves be misleading in that they would suggest too substantial a conception of the self.

Rorty, too, recognizes this ambiguity.[12] He points out how Nietzsche, having abandoned the traditional notion of truth,

> did not abandon the idea of discovering the causes of our being what we are. He did not give up the idea that an individual might track home the blind impress all his behavings bore. He only rejected the idea that this tracking was a process of discovery. In his view, in achieving this sort of self-knowledge we are not coming to know a truth that was out there (or in here) all the time. Rather, he saw self-knowledge as self-creation. The process of coming to know oneself, confronting one's contingency, tracking one's causes home, is identical with the process of inventing a new language—that is, of thinking up some new metaphors.[13]

[12] Rorty, *Contingency,* 27; see also p. 98.

[13] The distinction between the literal and the metaphorical, for Rorty, is essentially the distinction between customary ways of speaking and novel, idiosyncratic ways of speaking.

While Rorty is well aware that such "creation" is never *ex nihilo*, and that it is always conditioned by a language and culture that has been handed down to the seeker of autonomy,[14] his descriptions of the pursuit of autonomy emphasize the concept of self-creation to such an extent that it almost comes to seem as though there were no ambiguity at all. Thus his ironist is thoroughly nominalist and historicist, and does not believe that her judgments or her final vocabulary—the terms in which she describes her world and all that is important to her in that world—are candidates for truth in the traditional sense of truth as a relation between one's judgments and reality. In place of the traditional philosophical quest for truth Rorty describes the quest for a new, idiosyncratic vocabulary, which will liberate us from the final vocabularies that we have inherited as players of the language games that dominate our particular communities. When Rorty's ironist describes her quest for autonomy, then, "her description of what she is doing... is dominated by metaphors of making rather than finding, of diversification and novelty rather than convergence to the antecedently present. She thinks of final vocabularies as poetic achievements rather than as fruits of diligent inquiry according to antecedently formulated criteria."[15]

Meanwhile, even as Montaigne tells us that he cannot keep his subject still, and that he portrays passing rather than being, he also insists that "no man ever treated a subject he knew and understood better than I do the subject I have undertaken; and that in this I am the most learned man alive.... No man ever penetrated more deeply into his material, or plucked its limbs

[14] See Rorty, p.40-43.
[15] Rorty, *Contingency,* 77.

and consequences cleaner, or reached more accurately and fully the goal he had set for his work. To accomplish it, I need only bring it to fidelity; and...is in it, as sincere and pure as can be found" (III.2,611). Metaphors of discovery and fidelity clearly dominate the *Essais*. For Montaigne, ever greater degrees of autonomy, once achieved, are identical with ever greater degrees of self-knowledge. He does in some sense believe that he is discovering himself in his essays, and that there is a self to be discovered. Thus he writes in "Of repentance": "There is no one who, if he listens to himself, does not discover in himself a pattern all his own, a ruling pattern, which struggles against education and against the tempest of the passions that oppose it" (III:2,615).[16] So whereas Rorty emphasizes self-creation, Montaigne emphasizes self-discovery.

Ultimately, Rorty's emphasis on self-creation seems to be founded upon practical considerations. Thus he writes on the penultimate page of that book that "the only argument I could give for the views about language and about selfhood put forward in chapters 1 and 2 was that these views seemed to cohere better with the institutions of a liberal democracy than the available alternatives do. When the value of such institutions is challenged—not by practical proposals for the erection of alternative institutions but in the name of

[16] An interesting alternative to my argument that Montaigne does in some sense think that there is a self, some unity to be discovered by essaying himself, is Telma de Souza Birchal's thesis that Montaigne's identity is the product of his choice to construct a unified self out of the disparate actions, beliefs, and desires that he finds in his history. See Birchal, "Montaigne *impenitent*."

something more 'basic'—no direct answer can be given, because there is no neutral ground."[17]

Montaigne, on the other hand, does not explicitly explain his emphasis on the element of self-discovery in his project. And yet, it does seem to me that there are grounds for suggesting that his emphasis is theoretical in nature. For if we consider the *Essais* as a whole, we find that Montaigne clearly has a sense that the self is *sui generis* among the "objects" at which he aims his judgment. His self constantly changes, "not only by chance, but also by intention" (III:2,611), and yet it also remains the same (III:2,616,619). On the one hand he identifies his self with his thoughts (II:6,274), and yet on the other hand, he recognizes that he is his body: "Each one of my parts makes me myself just as much as every other one. And no other makes me more properly a man than this one [his penis]" (III:5,677). Finally, as we have seen, for Montaigne the self is that which, when observed, is modified; hence Starobinski's remark that for Montaigne, when it comes to the self, "the pleasure of looking is coupled with the pleasure of shaping."[18]

Since the self is *sui generis*, all descriptions of the self and the act of essaying the self must be understood analogically. But if this is the case, then deciding how to describe the self and the activity of essaying it will be a matter of determining which analogies hit the mark and to what extent. For essaying oneself, insofar as this is partially a matter of pursuing autonomy, does seem to bear a resemblance both to discovering something

[17] Rorty, *Contingency*, 197.
[18] Starobinski, 218.

antecedently there and yet also to constituting something not yet present at the outset of the project. But on the whole, it is clear that Montaigne finds that essaying himself is *more* like the former than the latter. One way of explaining why would be to say that in the latter activity the will plays a much more prominent role than it does in the former. Essaying begins with a deliberate decision. But beyond the decision to essay oneself, Montaigne does not deliberately steer himself in any given direction; that is, he does not aim to arrive at any particular beliefs or values. He does not have a model self that he is attempting to approximate. Once he gets going, his will takes a back seat to the eye of his judgment. This is not to say that it plays no role; the difference is one of degree, and this is why the act of essaying is somewhat ambiguous, and our descriptions of it, either in terms of self-discovery or self-creation, demand qualification. But again, on the whole, Montaigne's ways of describing his project clearly emphasize the element of self-discovery and self-revelation in all of this. Hence his emphasis the problem of self-knowledge: "I have seen no more evident monstrosity and miracle in the world than myself. We become habituated to anything strange by use and time; but the more I frequent myself and know myself, the more my deformity astonishes me, and the less I understand myself" (III:11,787).

Thus for all the similarities there are between their conceptions of autonomy and selfhood, the differences between Montaigne and Rorty run quite deep. For the emphasis that each lays on one particular element of the same philosophical act show that they have deeply opposed ways of understanding that act and its ambiguities. For Rorty, it would seem that ambiguity is a function of the language games we happen to play. If we transform the customary ways in which we speak about ourselves, we will change the rules of those games, and thereby diminish or eliminate the ambiguity. But for Montaigne, the ambiguity involved in essaying himself is the result of a truth about the reality of the self: that it is *sui generis*, and that when we try to give an account of it faithfully, we are led to say seemingly contradictory things, or at least things that require some qualification. Hence his famous line from the opening paragraphs of "Of repentance": "all in all, I may indeed contradict myself now and then; but truth, as Demades said, I do not contradict" (III:2,611).

In sum, then, for Montaigne the pursuit of autonomy is simultaneously practical and theoretical: it is a matter of actively constituting oneself, but it is also a matter of discovering the truth about oneself. What is distinctive about Montaigne's conception of moral autonomy is that it contains an eclectic combination of elements also found in prominent conceptions of autonomy from the ancient, modern, and postmodern eras of the history of Western philosophy. Montaigne, like Plato, takes the pursuit of autonomy to involve the theoretical attempt to discover truth. Like Kant, Montaigne thinks of autonomy as being a characteristic of one's judgment. And like Rorty, he takes autonomy to be a matter of making one's judgment one's own. Thus, for those who are on the one hand sympathetic to postmodern critiques of Platonic and Kantian conceptions of autonomy while on the other hand committed to a more traditional conception of truth and the self, Montaigne's conception of moral autonomy represents a theoretical and existential possibility well worth considering.

3

"Being a Citizen of No City": The *Essais* and the Political

Christine Dunn Henderson

Liberty Fund, Inc.

There are many reasons for which writing on the *Essais* and the political might, at first glance, appear odd. Most obviously, this could seem a topical mismatch because Montaigne appears at pains to distance himself from things political in the composition and content of the *Essais*. The story of how Montaigne resigned from the Bordeaux Parlement, retired to his study, and spent over a decade composing the *Essais* is well-known.[1] As with all things related to Montaigne, however, the "withdrawal" from public life is a bit more complicated than it seems, for during his withdrawal, Montaigne also served two terms as Mayor of Bordeaux (1581-1585) and advised various political figures, including Henry of Navarre. Those facts aside, it is true that Montaigne himself frames the *Essais* with the notion that his activity in composing them is a turn away from public life and from politics. His opening "Letter to the

---

[1] See Donald Frame, *Montaigne: A Biography* (New York: North Point Press, 1984) 114-115. Scholars, however, have debated whether Montaigne's withdrawal was genuine, disingenuous, or merely his iteration of a classical trope about retirement from public life in order to focus on the things of the mind. See, for example, Biancamaria Fontana, *Montaigne's Politics: Authority and Governance in the 'Essais'* (Princeton: Princeton University Press, 2008) 5.

Reader" proclaims that "I have set myself no goal but a domestic and private one. I have had no thought of serving either you or my own glory."[2]

Nevertheless, the *Essais* offer quite a bit which could be called political in a broad sense. This essay will explore three aspects of Montaigne's relationship to the political: 1. What does Montaigne teach us about politics? What kind of guidance does he offer us about good political life?; 2. What type of regime would be most conducive to Montaigne's?; and 3. What would a regime of Montaigne's look like? This final question contains two particularly interesting aspects: first, whether politics would exist in a world of Montaignes, and secondly, whether a world of Montaignes would be a community in any meaningful sense, or whether it would merely be a collection of independent individuals.[3] Having laid out the topics to be explored, one more thing is needed: a sort of a disclaimer. In keeping with the form and tenor of the *Essais*, this exploration of Montaigne and the political will make no—or very few—definitive statements. Instead, this essay hopes to explore a variety of possibilities, perhaps raising more questions than providing answers.

*****

[2] Montaigne, *The Complete Essays of Montaigne*, translated by Donald M. Frame (Stanford, CA: Stanford University Press, 1958) 2. All subsequent references to the *Essais* will be made within the text, with parenthetical page numbers referring to this edition.

[3] The first aspect of this final question has sparked considerable debate. Fontana, for example, argues that Montaigne is not political (Fontana, *Montaigne's Politics*, 144) whereas David Schaefer's *The Political Philosophy of Montaigne* (Ithaca: Cornell University Press, 1990) forcefully makes an opposing claim.

An investigation of what Montaigne teaches about the nature and shape of good political life can be subdivided into questions of form and content. Bracketing for a moment considerations of the regime's form, let us begin with content, where there are at least four things to be said about the type of politics of which Montaigne would approve. It seems appropriate to consider these four qualities before turning to form; although it might appear that Montaigne endorses certain qualities independent of the constitutional form (i.e., monarchy, republic, etc.), the qualities themselves may provide additional indications of the political form Montaigne prefers, all other things being equal.

First, Montaigne favors a *moderate* regime, one free both of the excesses of zealotry and of the extreme power relations of mastery and servitude. Given the importance Montaigne accords to the cultivation of individual judgment throughout the *Essais*, it is not surprising that he condemns the political and religious zealotry that distorts the judgment of "otherwise good men." Taken to the extreme, even good ideas and principles can become dangerous, and as Montaigne writes, "We can grasp virtue in such a way that it will become vicious, if we embrace it with too sharp and too violent a desire" (I:30,146). Zeal blinds men to the claims of reason and to their awareness of reason's limits; moreover, Montaigne tells us that excessive zeal draws men away from their proper home: themselves. Politically, Montaigne prefers the rivalry of Caesar and Pompey, to the "feverish factions" that had rent the France of his own day. The former, while bitter, maintained a certain moderation, preserving a degree of mutual respect and not carrying its parties into "furious and undiscerning hatred." By contrast, in the religious conflicts of sixteenth-century France, passion "entirely smothered" the "sense and understanding" of both sides; each group had become so blind to its rival's virtues and so blind to its own possible excesses (or prejudices) that eradication of the rival position seemed the only acceptable course—even at the expense of France's well-being—and moderate compromises such as mutual toleration had become unpalatable to either side (III:10,775).[4]

Montaigne's preference for a moderate politics also suggests a preference for non-absolute regimes, an inclination underlined by his repeated condemnations of mastery in all forms. "I have a distaste for mastery, both active and passive," he proclaims in "Of the disadvantage of greatness" (III:7,700). In various places in the *Essais*, Montaigne also jabs at "active mastery," associating the desire and act of commanding others with "imbecility" and drawing attention to the misery of monarchs, particularly absolute ones (e.g., I.42). Moreover, he casts a life governed by "strict and express command" as one opposed to nature,[5] and he notes that the act of commanding others removes us from ourselves. It seems that, as Thomas Jefferson would observe several centuries later, mastery is good neither for the master nor the slave. "Of Custom" adds its subtle dimension to Montaigne's attack on mastery, for that essay's elaborations of custom's power over men may be a first step in eliminating its passive mastery over humans; indeed, one project of the *Essais* seems to be the cultivation of an

[4] The fact that the longest chapter in the *Essais*, the "Apology for Raymond Sebond," endeavors to show the impossibility of absolute knowledge and thus can be read as an effort to neutralize religious zealotry by elevating doubt and skepticism further evidences the centrality of moderation in Montaigne's thoughts about politics.

[5] Or at least opposed to his own nature.

individual who is enslaved neither to another individual, nor to custom, nor to his own passions and desires, and who possesses an independence of judgment that renders him fit to govern himself.

Montaigne asserts that men should govern themselves before governing others, and whether in a political or private context, they should remain aware that all immoderate passions—including the political ones—draw them away from self-possession by distorting both reason and judgment (II:17,493; III:10,771). His skepticism about a politics of glory seems rooted in these same concerns. He terms glory a "vain phantom" (I:187) that renders its seekers dependent upon "erratic and unregulated" public opinion; in seeking glory, one abandons the self and reason, becoming wholly dependent upon fluctuating opinion and fortune (I:16,473). True glory, by contrast, consists in a tranquil life (I.16,71).[6]

Drawing upon these same threads, Montaigne also expresses skepticism about utopias and other grand—or, immoderate—political projects. As he tells the reader, "I am in the act of finishing up this man, not making another out of him..." (III:10,773). Visions of remaking are seductive yet dangerous, for they risk ignoring the limits and genuine possibilities of human nature in favor of an ideal, and they are prone to the same passionate excesses that lead reformers to destroy all that is, both good and bad, for the sake of a potentially unachievable vision. Montaigne's rejection of utopian politics, however, differs from the Machiavellianism which also dismisses those "imagined republics" that are so far from "what is," for while Machiavelli's anti-utopianism is coupled with a

---

[6] Montaigne suggests that the tranquil life is an individual and private pursuit.

hard-nosed *realpolitik*, Montaigne's many critiques of the Machiavellian politics of his day suggest that he also rejects a politics based solely on *raison d'état*.[7]

Following from the idea of moderation and the related concepts of anti-utopianism and anti-zealotry, the second quality that might be associated with a Montaignian politics is *toleration*. The importance of toleration to Montaigne's thought can be seen explicitly throughout the *Essais* as well as in the work's general character. In terms of direct textual arguments, the essay "Of freedom of conscience" holds a central place in the book, and there, Montaigne makes an unambiguous defense of toleration as a political policy.

What is perhaps most interesting about the *Essais'* treatment of the theme of tolerance, however, is the number of angles from which Montaigne mounts his defense. On the one hand are two pragmatic arguments in "Of freedom of conscience," the first drawn from the example of the Emperor Julian, who encouraged schism and faction as a means of keeping the people fighting amongst themselves so that they would not unite against him. The idea seems to be anachronistically akin to Madison's arguments about preventing majority faction through the multiplication of smaller factions. The second of Montaigne's pragmatic arguments on behalf of toleration is drawn from his own France, in which he claims that tolerant

[7] This is another major area of debate among Montaigne scholars, with the likes of Quentin Skinner and Nannerl Keohane locating Montaigne in the *raison d'état* tradition of Machiavelli, whereas Schaefer and others reject this. For representatives of each position, see Quentin Skinner, *The Foundations of Modern Political Thought, Vol. 1: The Renaissance* (Cambridge: Cambridge University Press, 1978) 253, and Robert J. Collins, "Montaigne's Rejection of Reason of State in 'De l'Utile et de l'honneste'" *Sixteenth Century Journal*, XXIII:1 (1992) 71-94.

policies "soften and relax them [faction and schism] through facility and ease," thus blunting "a point which is sharpened by rarity, novelty and difficulty" (II:19,509). If opposition is strengthened because it is repressed, the wise political course is one of toleration, in the name of stability and preservation.

On the other hand is the principled argument, with Montaigne noting the virtual impossibility of ever achieving rational certainty about things spiritual and other-worldly. Supporting this is Montaigne's pre-Lockean awareness that political remedies and tactics cannot change faith: in short, faith cannot be compelled. Man can attempt to enlighten opinion, but he cannot change judgment or belief: "God holds your heart and will provide you with your choice" (III:11,791). In the end, choice rests with the individual, who must "sift" through and weigh the evidence he finds (II:17,500), choosing the truth for himself.

There are also several more general aspects of Montaigne's thought that augment his non-pragmatic case for toleration. First is the elevation of doubt and skepticism throughout the *Essais*. Perhaps the most prominent qualities of the *Essais*, doubt and skepticism serve as antidotes to the arrogance of "certainty" which would impose itself upon others. Not only are these qualities manifested by Montaigne through his very essaying activity and thus given a practical endorsement, but his preference for doubt and skepticism is also repeatedly made explicit. In "Of cripples," for example, he reminds his reader of the fact that he talks "about everything by way of conversation, and about nothing by way of advice" (III:11,790)—perhaps because of understanding's "supple and erratic" nature (III:11,792)—and he recommends the Augus-tinian stance that "it is better to lean toward doubt than toward assurance in things difficult to prove and dangerous to believe" (III:11,789-90). Montaigne's reminders of worldly things' diversity and of the fact that custom and nature are based on the variable (and fallible) judgments of individuals serve similar purposes in promoting toleration. Added to this is the idea of an extensive private sphere—in which the individual is free to act and believe as s/he wishes—which permeates Montaigne's entire *oeuvre*. Finally, the highly individualized individual depicted in the *Essais* stands as an endorsement of variety and thus of toleration; combined with the presence of a robust private sphere, individuality works against ideas of standardization and intolerance, and in favor of variety and peaceful coexistence.[8]

Although Montaigne opposes dogmatism and endorses individuality, he is not opposed to regularity, particularly when it comes to the law. *Rule of law*, then, is another characteristic of good politics in the Montaignian sense.[9] Not only must the laws be impartial (applying equally to all), but they also must be generally known and intelligible to all. These points lie at the heart of Montaigne's critique of the French legal system in "Of experience" (III.13) and "Of custom" (I.23). There, Montaigne takes French law to task for what he sees as its deliberate incomprehensibility; not only has the combination of feudal law overlaid upon Roman foundations produced a system incomprehensible to ordinary citizens, but the laws themselves are written in Latin, rather than in the language of

[8] The theme of individuality and a robust private sphere is threaded throughout the *Essais*. See below. See also Schaefer, especially chapter 11, and Nannerl O. Keohane, "Montaigne's Individualism," *Political Theory*, 5:3 (August, 1977) 363-390.

[9] This phrasing is provisional and begs the question of whether politics is in any sense desirable for Montaigne. We will return to this broader question later.

those governed by them (II:23,85). Moreover, the abstruse character of legal writing itself—an early legalese—increased the average citizen's (or even the above-average citizen's) difficulty in understanding the laws that govern him.[10] Language, writes Montaigne, "so easy for any other use, becomes obscure and unintelligible in contracts and wills." This leads to doubt and contradiction, which in turn spawn various and varied interpretations of the law; in the end, the multiplicity of interpretations "disperse and shatter" truth (and justice), rendering it as ungraspable as quicksilver slipping through children's fingers (III:13,816).

In addition to these linguistic features, Montaigne criticizes French law for its intricacy, particularly for the overlapping layers of law—some obsolete and some contradictory—and for the law codes' over-specificity. In terms of the laws' contradictions, he notes that while the nobility's code of honor requires an insult be avenged by action, the civil code criminalizes the same action; with such incongruities, the citizen can hardly be likely to discern general notions of justice, much less to follow them. In terms of the proliferation of laws, Montaigne observes that "We have in France more laws than all the rest of the world together,"—a "hundred thousand" laws for a hundred thousand actions (III:13,815). Yet laws are by nature general, and thus this superabundance has neither provided rules for every action of every individual, nor has it done anything to curtail judicial caprice. Instead of curbing judicial discretion, "there was never such a powerful and licentious freedom" (III:13,815). To these complaints, Montaigne adds the charges that "judging is sold" and that French legal

[10] Fontana, *Montaigne's Politics,* 27.

practices demand a fee for the dispensation of justice, thus placing the poor at a disadvantage.

By contrast with the prevailing French practices, a "Montaignian" polity would be characterized by the impartial administration of justice, and the rule of few rather than more laws—easily understood, equally applied, and equally binding upon all.

But what would the *character* of such a regime be? This brings us to the question of Montaigne's conservatism, a matter of considerable contention in the scholarship.[11] Is Montaigne or is he not conservative when it comes to politics? This, I think, is rather difficult to settle. So much of Montaigne is innovative, from the nature of his essaying activity to outright statements such as "I seek out change indiscriminately and tumultuously. My style and my mind alike go roaming" (III:9,761). As readers of Montaigne, we celebrate the innovativeness that lies at the very heart of his project. Yet, he often evinces a conservative streak, particularly in matters political. How might we make sense of this apparent tension?

The *Essais'* discussions of custom are particularly interesting in this context of conservatism versus innovation, for they mirror some of the complexities of Montaigne's own position. On the one hand, the discussions on custom endeavor to separate what is merely customary (practice) from what is considered natural and thus to facilitate the transcendence of custom and change. On the other hand, in underscoring custom's considerable power in men's lives, Montaigne

---

[11] For example, Fontana and Schaefer stand at opposite ends of this debate, with Fontana following the more traditional line which casts Montaigne as a conservative skeptic, and Schaefer asserting that Montaigne is a deep reformer in conservative's clothing.

reminds us of the difficulty—and indeed, often the undesirability—of change. Custom, then, is indeed "the queen and empress of the world" (I:23,83), but she is a monarch whose powers have both advantages and disadvantages. Although custom may prevent us from accessing the natural via reflection and reason, it is not necessarily or even generally true that Montaigne thinks the customary should be jettisoned. For example, custom may preserve liberty, in that custom seems to be responsible for a free people's hatred of non-republican forms.[12] Moreover, Montaigne tells us he is "disgusted with innovation," and he expresses doubts that the benefits of changing *any* accepted law will ever outweigh the disadvantages of changing it (I:23,86). Fear of unbridled political change permeates the *Essais*; as but one example, he writes, "...in public affairs there is no course so bad, provided it is old and stable, that is not better than change and commotion.... because of the difficulty of improving our condition and the danger of everything crumbling to bits, if I could put a spoke in our wheel and stop it at this point, I would do so with all my heart..." (II:17,497).[13] Elsewhere, Montaigne notes that the individual's duty to existing political orders, however defective, is "to suffer them patiently...to conceal their vices, to abet them by commending their indifferent actions if their authority

---

[12] Reading "Of custom" in conjunction with Tocqueville's discussions of general ideas shows the former's influence upon the latter.

[13] "Of vanity" seems to mirror this political conservatism on the more personal level. Speaking of his father, Montaigne writes, "I love to follow his example and his rules, and shall bind my successors to them as much as I can...I glory in the fact that his will still operates and acts through me" (726). In reading this passage, however, one might keep in mind Montaigne's account of deliberately distancing himself from his father's example in the conduct of his own political life.

needs our support" (I:3,9).[14] Passages such as these, or the fears of radical change expressed (III.9,731), give us a more conservative Montaigne.

Yet other passages suggest Montaigne has a moderate stance on political change and reform, including the ending of "Of custom," in which Montaigne concedes that reform is the appropriate course in certain situations. Rather than let revolution destroy a country, it would "perhaps be more wisely done to lower your head and give a little to the blow" by reforming the laws, for "It would be better to make the laws will what they can do, since they cannot do what they will" (I;23,89).[15] Finally, there is the nature of the *Essais* themselves, which is innovative in so many ways and which suggests a Montaigne who embraces change.

The picture is indeed complicated. But why does the degree of Montaigne's conservatism matter? There are various reasons, but one is that this issue may have some bearing on the form of the regime. Does Montaigne have a clear preference for one regime over another? What can we learn about his preferences from the *Essais*? Essentially, this is the question of whether Montaigne prefers republics to monarchies.

Textually—and with caveats about Montaigne's recommendations in favor of preserving the existing regime, whether a monarchy or a republic—most of the evidence suggests a preference for republics. This preference begins with Montaigne's several comments indicating the essential equality among men (II.12). Montaigne asserts that it is Fortune and

---

[14] See also the exhortation to obey an existing regime, even if defective, in the "Apology" (II.12).

[15] See also III.9; like "Of custom," it can be read as both pro-change and pro-stasis.

not inherent superiority which elevates some to great positions (II:17,479); thus, while convention and habit cause men to distinguish between kings and commoners, kings possess no inherent merit upon which claims to rule or of obedience might rest. As he writes, "We owe subjection and obedience equally to all kings, for that concerns their office; but we do not owe esteem, any more than affection, except to their office" (I:3,9). Elsewhere, Montaigne reminds his reader that the prince serves by the good will of the people, thereby suggesting the importance of consent rather than claims of birth or of any inherent superiority. Viewed rightly, kings and commoners are fundamentally the same; strip the trappings of his office away like "coats of paint," says Montaigne, remove the king from his "stilts," and he becomes simply another man, with the same virtues and vices of body and soul that plague any other man. Convention makes and magnifies inequalities, whereas the "natural and original condition" is one in which emperors and porters are virtually indistinguishable. "Of cannibals" also suggests that equality is the natural human condition, for the cannibals' untouched society has "no name for political superiority, [and] no custom of servitude" (I:31,153). By noting that the original condition of the cannibals surpasses the golden age of the ancient poets, Montaigne seems to suggest that a condition of political equality, such as a republic, is best.[16]

[16] Of course, these same natural cannibals eat their fellow humans, which might lead one to question the status of "natural." Nevertheless, it seems safe to say that as a whole, the natural holds a privileged place in *Essais*. Thus, the cannibals are less a blueprint for reform than an indication of the direction such reform might take (Schaefer, *Political Philosophy of Montaigne,* 198).

"Of the inequality that is between us" and "Our feelings reach out beyond us" offer further comparisons of the relative merits of monarchies and republics. In these essays, Montaigne appears at pains to elaborate upon the disadvantages and inconveniences of monarchy: on the monarch's side is loneliness, being spied upon, having every action over-analyzed and judged, and lack of friendship ("wherein consists the sweetest and most perfect fruit of human life" [II:42,195]), while on the people's side, undue deference and a false belief in the ruler's superiority prevent them from using approbation and disapprobation to check his excessive behavior and caprice. Montaigne also suggests that ruling the self should precede ruling others, and because the monarchs Montaigne sketches seem incapable of self-rule, their claims to rule others are further eroded. To this, we might add the call in "Of vanity" for "more proportion between the command and the obedience," which could be read as some endorsement for democratic governance. In one of his most direct statements on the form of government, Montaigne asserts that despite his dislike of some of democracy's own excesses, particularly when resulting from superstition or religious zeal, democracy nevertheless "seems" to him "the most natural and equitable" form of government (12). Understood as self-rule, democratic and republican government also solve the problem of mastery, for one is not enslaved to oneself or to the representatives one elects.[17]

We begin to see indications that Montaigne favors democracies or democratic republics, but as with all statements about Montaigne, this picture is not one without qualifications. The

[17] Schaefer, *Political Philosophy of Montaigne*, 375.

passage just quoted from "Our feeling reach out beyond us" about democracy's naturalness is really the qualifying phrase to the main statement: "I am almost ready to vow irreconcilable hatred to democratic rule" (12).[18] Elsewhere, Montaigne highlights the need in all polities for some form of "empty ceremony or of lying opinion to serve as a curb to keep the people in their duty" (477). It would appear, then, that the people oscillate between not wishing to concern themselves with public life and not wishing to exercise their power rationally or moderately; thus, popular government might not be desirable or even possible in any long-term sense. In addition to these explicit reservations about popular government, Montaigne's conservative strain and his criticisms of political innovation could lead him to have reservations about democracy's potentially frequent reverses. On the other hand, the idea that democratic government makes—to anticipate Tocquevillian language—"retrievable mistakes" seems to fit nicely with Montaigne's skepticism or with his provisional world view.

"Of vanity" further complicates this question of regime preference, for while Montaigne does appear to have some broad preference for popular government, "Of vanity" suggests neutrality on form. "Not in theory, but in truth, the best and most excellent government for each nation is the one under which it has preserved its existence. Its form and essential fitness depend on habit" (III:9,731). While this passage can obviously be read as evidence of Montaigne's conservatism, another plausible interpretation points to a certain relativism about regime form and to the idea that different regimes are

[18] *Almost*, but not quite.

appropriate for different peoples and different moments in a nation's life.[19] Perhaps the form matters less than the content or tone, and perhaps Montaigne is less interested in the question of who holds power than he is in the character of the rule; perhaps it matters less whether one lives under a democratic or a monarchical government, and more whether that government is legal, moderate, non-zealous, non-radical, and tolerant.

But there is a final wrinkle before leaving this question of regime form, and even this suggestion of neutrality regarding regime needs some qualification in light of the "project" of the *Essais*, which seems to be—explicitly, several times—the cultivation of individual judgment in the name of a particular type of autonomy. If the cultivation of individual judgment and the development of individual autonomy is indeed the *Essais'* project or even one aspect of its intention, then it would seem that the more people practice the judgment-honing, essaying activity Montaigne seems both to model and to recommend, the less likely they are to accept received authority that does not emanate from them and to which they have not explicitly consented. Perhaps, after all, there is a firm preference for political self-government, provided it has the moderate character Montaigne endorses.[20]

Moving away from whether Montaigne offers any guidance about the form and content of a good regime, the theme of Montaigne and the political can be turned in a different direction, to ask what regime would be most conducive to

---

[19] "Of custom" can be read both in support of this suggestion and in tension with it.

[20] Here, one might also consider Montaigne's pride at being given honorary Roman citizenship.

Montaignes. Specifically, let us turn the question of monarchies versus republics on this point, and here, we have some interesting shades or nuances to what we have already seen about the relative merits of these two forms.

As we have seen, republics seem the most natural—and possibly the best—form of government. Nevertheless, it is difficult to imagine that a world of classical republicanism would be friendly to Montaignes. The onus of political and civic duty would probably prohibit the kind of private activity to which Montaigne devotes himself in the *Essais*. Indeed, it is difficult to imagine how a citizen actively devoted to participating in the polity's governance would find time to devote himself to Montaigne's essaying activity. To be sure, Montaigne did not find that his own activity precluded political engagement, and we know that he served twice as mayor of Bordeaux during the so-called "retirement" during which he wrote the *Essais*. We will return to that not insignificant biographical detail in a moment, but despite his own political service, Montaigne seems to warn of extensive political commitments, telling his reader, "We must husband the freedom of our soul and mortgage it only on the right occasions" (III:10,767).[21] Apparently, then, the classical republican model is out, as it would demand more from the individual soul than Montaigne would care to give.

The *Essais* does, however, suggest that it is possible to engage in politics without over-mortgaging the soul's freedom. Through Montaigne's account of his own political career, both as political advisor and his role as elected official, a model of political engagement emerges that is not destructive of the

[21] This quotation's context is political.

individual's identity or liberty. "Of the useful and the honorable" gives us Montaigne's account of his ability to serve kings disinterestedly and without deceit—without change in behavior or character, and without departing from his natural or free self. In "Of husbanding your will," Montaigne recounts his election as mayor of Bordeaux, an election that took place in his absence and without any desire on his part to hold office. Despite his lack of political ambition, Montaigne was unable to refuse the election, due to royal involvement in the process. Upon assuming the office, Montaigne claims that he "deciphered himself" to the gentlemen of Bordeaux exactly as he understood himself—"without memory, without vigilance, without experience, and without vigor; also without hate, without ambition, without avarice, and without violence"—and that this self-description contained within it what they might expect from his tenure in office. He also announced to them that he would not allow the cares of the office to weigh as heavily upon him as they had on his father, whose soul had been "cruelly agitated by this public turmoil," and whose public-spiritedness had been greater than his care for himself.

Montaigne's approach to politics differed from his father's and flowed directly from those announced character traits, as well as from the simplicity, lack of artifice, and the easy-going or tolerant nature he claims (II:17,483-4,487). Montaigne tells us that, as mayor, he was non-zealous and tolerant in the religious controversies raging at the time, exercising the powers of his office both minimally and impartially, and also not allowing his own interests and beliefs to blind himself to the opposing parties' claims and merits. All of this is consistent with what we have already seen Montaigne finds characteristic of good politics. The politics modeled through his own political activity was, moreover, a minimalist government, for Montaigne's administration was said to have left no mark or trace on Bordeaux and to have been a regime of abstention and conservation rather than one of activity.[22]

Such a regime would appear to be best for both the polity and the individual. Montaigne suggests that we should only give ourselves minimally and rarely to the management of others' affairs, and by following the minimalist, tolerant, conserving, and lethargic model of government Montaigne's own political activity depicts, the individual's soul can remain in repose, its freedom not mortgaged to the demands of the common good. If love of one's own was the political problem confronted by the Ancients, love of one's own seems the solution for Montaigne, for the "problem" is a politics that requires us to care more for the good of the community than for ourselves, and which thus removes us from "friendship with ourselves." Montaigne suggests that a certain kind of minimalist politics is able to avoid the problem of dividing us. Under such a politics, Montaigne says, "I have been able to take part in public office without departing one nail's breadth from myself, and to give myself to others without taking myself from myself" (III:10,770).[23]

A modern model, then, begins to emerge from these descriptions—"modern" in the sense later employed by Benjamin Constant, to describe a regime that privileges the individual over the community and that stakes out a considerable private sphere for individual freedom. Among other things, the modern regime endorses freedom of

[22] "That's a good one!" says Montaigne of such a regime (III:781).

[23] The account of his father's political life is the most obvious point of contrast.

expression broadly, but perhaps most importantly for our purposes in considering the *Essais*, it leaves the shaping of the individual's character to the individual. The modern regime is based upon the understanding that pursuit of the good life is not the goal of political life; rather, it is an essentially private and individualized—though not necessarily solitary—activity. "The main responsibility of each of us is his own conduct, and that is what we are here for," (III:10,769-70) writes Montaigne. A politics corresponding to this would be necessarily have a minimalist public sphere and an extensive private sphere, for it would acknowledge that the individual is the best judge of his/her own good.[24]

If modernity is the key to a politics supportive of Montaignes, this does not settle the question of regime form, for it also seems possible that a "modern" monarchy might also be conducive to Montaignes. Perhaps a modern monarchy would be even more conducive to Montaignes than a modern republic, for the monarchy might surpass the republic in relieving individuals of the burden of devoting any time to public affairs. Like the modern republic, however, such a "modern monarchy" would have to leave Montaignes unmolested to pursue their own activities, and it would have to steer clear of the monarchical tendency to impose uniformity upon the many things and people of whose differences Montaigne so often reminds us. It would have to be a skeptical monarchy, if possible, which would not be overly concerned with changing its judgments when warranted, but which would

---

[24] A contrasting interpretation sees Montaigne's skepticism about the possibilities of politics as evidence of his rejection of the modern political project. See Ann Hartle, *Michel de Montaigne: Accidental Philosopher* (Cambridge: Cambridge University Press, 2003) 220-226.

also not change things too frequently. If such a monarchy could exist, and provided it had the characteristics we have already seen—moderation, rule of law, etc., as well as a considerable private sphere, no censorship, a high degree of freedom of speech and freedom of worship—it could end up being the regime that would leave to private individuals the greatest degree of freedom to lead the lives they judged best.

To be sure, those are some pretty big "ifs" with regard to monarchies, but overall, the point is that, in terms of its ability to produce or sustain Montaignes, the regime's form matters less than its scope, or its modern character.

Having now said something—or rather, some things, some very indefinite things—about content and form, let us turn the question of Montaigne and politics slightly differently, by asking what a regime of Montaignes would look like. There are a number of ways in which this final theme might be considered, but they all come down to the question of whether politics would exist in any deep or significant sense in a world of Montaignes. From this question, we will touch on the question of what a community of Montaignes might look like and, finally, to the related question of whether or not "a community of Montaignes" is a contradiction in terms.

Here again, it is worthy of remark that both Montaigne's own public service and the presence of political figures in the *Essais* suggest that a world of Montaignes need not be a world entirely devoid of politics. In other words, a world of Montaignes would not necessarily be the world of the cannibals, whose society is familial or tribal rather than political. Nevertheless, Montaigne reveals—both explicitly and through the act of writing the *Essais*, which depicts a private life—his preference for the private life over a public/political one. As a whole, the *Essais* privilege the private sphere over the public one, and while politics might be a feature of a community of Montaignes, it would not be that community's defining characteristic; a community of Montaignes might require a minimalist politics in order to coordinate service provision or basic defense, but politics would always be secondary. Whatever Montaigne's ultimate project is—perhaps the cultivation of individual judgment and autonomy, or in the language of III.10, "finishing a man"—political life is neither a means to that end, nor the arena in which that project might best be executed.[25]

Montaigne tells us this repeatedly. While he is literally "a citizen of no city" (III:9,766), his self-description could also be taken figuratively, to suggest that political affiliation is no essential element of an individual like Montaigne. If—with the exception of political life modeled after Montaigne's own service—political service is numbered among the many things that divert and distract us from ourselves,[26] the implication is that the private sphere is more important. In essays such as "Of vanity," Montaigne opposes political life to freedom (III:9,761); together with the association between freedom and nature, one might draw the conclusion that, unless carefully constructed to allow the individual to engage in politics without departing from himself (as outlined in Montaigne's accounts of his own political activity), political life is both unfree and unnatural. The best life is *not* the shared pursuits of political life; if we are to believe Montaigne, the best life orients

[25] This is but one of the senses in which Montaigne is clearly modern.
[26] Including market activity.

entirely around the individual. And what could be better than the private life as he describes it in "Of presumption":

> The world always looks straight ahead; as for me, I turn my gaze inward, I fix it there and keep it busy. Everyone looks in front of him; as for me, I look inside me; I have no business but with myself; I continually observe myself, I take stock in myself, I taste myself… [A]s for me, I roll about in myself (II. 17; 499).

As Nannerl Keohane notes, Montaigne "succeeded better than any other writer in making such a self-centered life attractive, in teaching men to think of individualism as a satisfactory and appealing norm." The ideal of an individual whose self and private commitments are privileged lies at the core of modernity –and of Montaigne's own modernity—"against the ancient ideal of the engaged citizen and the medieval ideal of the self-sacrificing saint."[27]

If a world of Montaignes would not be primarily a political community, we are still left with the question of whether a world of Montaignes would be a community in any meaningful sense, or whether it would be merely a collection of independent individuals. It is true that the Montaigne revealed to us in the *Essais* is a particular individual, revealed to the readers in all of his endearing and bizarre idiosyncrasies, but if all individuals were similarly stripped down, would we find some common core from which a human community might arise? Here, the answer seems a pretty straightforward "yes," and because a complete treatment of this question goes well beyond the scope of this paper, I merely want to sketch by way

[27] Keohane, "Montaigne's Individualism," 366.

of conclusion why a world of Montaignes could be something more than an assembling of atomized individuals. To draw upon Montaigne's words and put the matter simply, the cannibals who seem to represent nature at its more uncorrupted state live in a community—they are not hermits. Moreover, despite the praise of solitude in I.39, Montaigne himself does not reject society. The Montaigne presented to the reader of the *Essais* is both sociable and a lover of discussions, and Montaigne avows that "There is nothing to which nature seems to have inclined us more than to society" (I:28,136). Some type of community or society then, seems both natural to and good for man, and while we are each individuals, we are individuals whose existences are naturally and fundamentally intertwined with other individuals. This suggests that beneath all of our individualized idiosyncrasies, we share something that makes us intelligible to each other[28] and that makes us, perhaps, necessary to or good for each other.

Stepping back from the text of the *Essais* and considering Montaigne's stripping down activity in essaying himself, that activity is one which is in some sense private or which requires privileging the private over the public, yet it ends up being a shared activity. On one level, that activity is shared because the *Essais* are published by Montaigne himself, in more than one edition during his lifetime, and because we feel in Montaigne's essaying activity a kind of conversation going on, both with himself and with us, as his readers. In another sense, by revealing himself to his readers as he is, Montaigne models an openness which may "inspire a common trust—a trust rooted not in a common goal but in the recognition that the other

[28] Even if only an awareness that we are all idiosyncratic.

fellow is no greater than oneself, and that the pleasures one person seeks need not be incompatible with others' enjoyment."[29]

One model of the kind of natural community—or communities—that would be based on openness, trust, and mutual pleasure and that could emerge in a world of Montaignes is friendship.[30] *Essais* I.28, the essay devoted to Montaigne's friendship with Étienne de La Boétie, depicts friendship as the kind of community that does not involve questions of mastery and subordination and that could exist among natural individuals, without sacrifice of freedom from any member of such a community. Perfect friendship is said to be the blending of two souls, in which there is no distinction between the self and the friend. Unlike the blending of the individual self into the political order, however, the blurring of friend and self entails no loss or sacrifice of the self's freedom. Rather, true friendship is said to be a perfect unity, in which the friends' souls "mingle and blend with each other so completely that they efface the seam that joined them, and cannot find it again" (I:28,139). Such friendship is predicated upon the freedom of the individual's soul, yet it enhances the soul's refinement, thus also increasing its freedom. Montaigne tells us that he is "finishing a man," and while an individual's pursuit of that end is a matter for private life rather than for politics, it is

---

29 Schaefer, *Political Philosophy of Montaigne*, 335.

30 See Michael Allen Gillespie, "Montaigne's Humanistic Liberalism" (*The Journal of Politics*, 47:1 [Feb., 1985], 140-159) for the argument that Montaigne revises the Aristotelian understanding of friendship as supporting the *polis*, offering instead a model of friendship with the self, as "the source of self-knowledge and indeed of the self itself" (146). Though different, my point about the possibility of community within a world of Montaignes is not necessarily in tension with this interpretation.

nevertheless a pursuit which can be undertaken—and is possibly best undertaken—in the company of one's other self, in the non-political community of friendship.

4

"How to Get Drunk: A Practical Guide for the Perplexed (Or, On Michel de Montaigne's 'Of Drunkenness')"

Eduardo Velásquez

I.

"How to Get Drunk: A Practical Guide for the Perplexed" is a title for persons who seek illumination as they stumble through life trying to be of use to others and happy for themselves. "On Michel de Montaigne's 'Of drunkenness'" provides some initial assurances for serious scholars (say those pondering the meaning of philosophy or defining the "genre" of the Essays) that the author pursues an intellectual topic worthy of their consideration.

Moral and intellectual virtue is not so easily combined, however. Those of us who work at universities know that the "life of the mind" is not possible without the aid of intoxicants. Drunkenness has for long been associated with the academy. And it enjoys the endorsement of a man reputed the wisest among philosophers in the Western canon. In a dialogue entitled *Laws*, Socrates, in the voice of an "Athenian Stranger," says to the astonishment of his young interlocutors that good regimes may require well-regulated drink. The crafty gadfly is at it again in Plato's Symposium (and "symposium" literally means "drinking party"). Gathered with a few respectable and not so respectable youths over a few jugs, Socrates tells how he learned *eros* or love of wisdom from the seer Diotima. Philosophy is akin to drunkenness.

To have social and academic life conjoined and blessed by so eminent an authority is liberating. Although, I must say, Socrates' exhortations to drink are wanting. Howsoever eloquent the praise of Dionysus, no Google search of the dialogues comes up with Socratic instructions on how much to drink, when and how. Wine seems to be the preferred intoxicant. *In vino veritas*. But what of some practical advice for those who want to get down to business? A few clicks on the "I'm Feeling Lucky" button and *voilà*. Up pops Michel de Montaigne's "Of drunkenness." I scrolled through the first few pages. Lo and behold, this Sixteenth Century nobleman takes up where Socrates leaves off. Within a few pages I hear Montaigne asking the right questions: whether it is preferable to chug as the Germans do (avoiding the inconvenience of tasting bad wines because good wines aren't always at hand), whether to taste a savory glass full or two with meals, as the French do (giving ponderous discourses over the potential health benefits of the fermented grape, as do our contemporaries), whether to share drink generously with friends and enemies (loosening their tongues so they may divulge their secrets), and not forgetting the philosophers, whether wine on a full or empty stomach makes them more lusty for the exercise of love.

Readers may wonder why I search for answers on the Internet rather than in my experience. Truth is, I am not constitutionally well endowed for drink. Holding (or as the case may be, not holding) my liquor well has not hampered my zeal for philosophy, however. The day before I was scheduled to deliver a lecture on Montaigne at Mercer University, I went out into the field in search of empirical evidence of Socrates' wisdom.[1] No more auspicious day could I have selected for my researches. The evening before my lecture on Montaigne, Mercer University was abuzz. Their men's basketball team was playing in a national championship. Not the "Final Four." Better, I was told, the CIT (CollegiateInsider.com Post-Season Tournament) final. Coinciding as it did with the equally anticipated weekend conference on Montaigne set the stage for the union of intelligence and happiness.

Whether it was in the sixth or seventh establishment I frequented that evening, I honestly don't remember. I had been bar hopping all night because no one seemed eager to discuss the meaning of philosophy. The young scholar who agreed to the interrogation assured me that failure to engage his peers had nothing to do with the topic. A few methodological changes would suffice, among them, that I drop the clipboard, ditch the L.L. Bean tweed jacket, dye my grey hair brown and gravitate to the darker sections of the bar in search of interview subjects. Not to sound ungrateful, I thanked the young scholar. Some light chatter about the superiority of the CIT to the Final Four ensued. Seeing that we agreed on the relative merits of each, we turned to the real thing.

Asked whether drinking was compatible with higher learning, the subject responded with a bellowing laugh that

[1] A version of this essay was performed at Mercer University, in celebration of the Fifth Annual Conference on Great Books and Ideas, March 28, 2012. No intoxicants were served during academic discussions (but should have). I must nonetheless thank Charlie Thomas and Will Jordan for their gracious invitation. All errors that undoubtedly abound throughout are due to my engagements elsewhere.

triumphed imperiously over the conversations of his fellow intellectuals. In the suspenseful silence of his laughter's aftermath (it was so arresting that it silenced every other voice), the young scholar said somewhat sarcastically: "You call this drinking?" During the ten minutes we'd been together the subject had taken two shots and chased each down with a draft. To the best of my understanding, that is called drinking. Apparently not. In a slurred voice rising above the hum of Snoop Dogg's *Doggfather* playing on the corner jukebox, the young scholar said, and I quote: "This here is not drinking. This here is 'pre-game.'"

"Pre-game" was not until then in my drinking lexicon. Partial as I am to learning, I asked the young scholar for a definition. One was forthcoming, he said, but not before "I put this where it belongs." Like a hawk swooping down for prey, the poncho-wearing lad sporting a tattoo of a bear on his forearm whisked a shot glass from atop the mahogany bar and flung it down his throat in a single gulp. He then turned to me with a puzzled look. My keen acuity borne of may hours in the field allowed me to surmise: the bartender had not prepared a chaser. The young scholar drones on in a lecturing tone that it is impossible to sustain a serious conversation in the absence of drink. Just as Socrates had predicted. Imitating the tone the young scholar's slurred voice for effect, I ordered a round for my research assistant and his companions at the symposium (on my questionnaire I dutifully reminded myself to include the research expense in my reimbursement). The establishment was awash in gregarious conversation and I was suddenly the center of attention. No better recreation of a Socratic symposium could be found anywhere.

"So, tell me, what is pre-game," I asked. With eloquence and aplomb the young scholar said that he had been left behind after his friends trekked to Utah State to watch the game. "The 'Aggies' hold home court advantage," he said nervously. The young scholar remained on campus for the extra credit points attendance at a conference the next day would earn him. For the diligence of scholar just like him, the university generously prepared several locations for the intellectual community to watch the game on large TV screens. For "technical reasons" the young scholar uttered but I could not quite comprehend, the events were supposedly "dry." With a glare of incredulity and indignation toward me, the young scholar did not spare me his opinion of these restrictions: "How are we supposed to enjoy ourselves?" Indeed, not unlike campuses across America, faculty and administrators have abandoned Socratic ideals.

By now I understood that these questions were not unlike those posed by university professors, that is, rhetorical, of no import save to interrupt the monotony of their own voice. I waited in dutiful anticipation. True to the spirit of Socrates, the young scholar said that drink permits them to "engage fully" in the spirit of the event. The administration, he added, is always preoccupied with less than full engagement. Done in right way, "pre-game" lasts long enough to arrive at "post-game." To which I responded in earnest: "Is the 'post-game' my lecture on Michel de Montaigne tomorrow morning?" In French perfected by a slurred Southern drawl, the young scholar said: "Mais qui, bien sur!"

II.

At the small "elite" liberal arts college I happily call home, the custom of drinking before drinking is called "front-loading." I must admit this makes me a bit envious of students at Mercer. Being myself constitutionally more disposed to happiness than work, "pre-game" sounds better. I don't blame students at my home campus for their rhetoric, though. They have as much choice over their customs as we do ours. "Front-loading" is a term engrained in campus culture. It speaks to a tradition cemented over generations. Some decades back students at a small liberal arts college where I teach voted themselves (if I understand the methods of the Princeton Review correctly) the happiest (or most inebriated, if you pardon the redundancy) and the brightest (or most intelligent). And that was before the Administration got serious about drinking. Don't take my word for it. My commitment to empirical research and data is irreproachable, as you now know. Daniel de Vise of the Washington Post (May 22, 2012) summarized the latest finding of National Survey for Student Engagement. Among the colleges and universities in the state of Virginia, he ranks my home campus among the best. Employing the same method as the Princeton Review, students responded to a survey asking them to account for the number of hours they studied per week—twenty on average. The *Washington Post* reporter was as encouraged by his findings as were Administration Officials. One university high-ranking source, quoted by de Vise, said: "There's something to a campus culture." Emphasizing the influence of faculty over campus climate he added: "You can't invent it and you can't radically change it."

Ask any Washington and Lee student to capture the defining characteristics of their culture and most will invariably say: "Play Hard, Work hard." It is the closest thing we have to a mantra. Only the other day I heard a crowd of about forty students attending our school's Division III playoff football game chanting it. On a student blog post I read that "Play Hard, Work Hard" is sung at fraternity and sorority initiations. Perhaps the best sign of the marriage of intellectual and moral virtue is the Admissions Office. Repeatedly I hear the mantra sung by sorority sisters giving campus tours (walking backwards in high heels while simultaneously speaking forward, as does Chris Martin in the Coldplay "The Scientist" video, a feat impossible to believe unless you had seen it on YouTube). I wouldn't be surprised if we dropped the university motto "Non Incautus Futuri" (Not Unmindful of the Future) in favor of "Ludere Dura, Studere Difficile." No more urgent need for a university committee exists than this.

I am told that back in the day, the mantra used to be "Play Hard, Study Hard." Administrative initiatives safeguarding the integrity of liberal education by vetting syllabi by a committee of former accrediting agency employees prompted the change. Peruse the course menu of an incoming student ordering up a full four-course "work-load." Let's say this Freshman (or "First-Year" as I am now required to say due to recent administrative committee changes to official campus rhetoric) starts by signing up for English composition, "Shakespeare: Text and Context." On the menu for the term: six plays and six fifteen hundred-word essays. By decree of the Associate Vice-President for Institutional Effectiveness, a course with "six papers" is designated "Writing Intensive." And all "Writing Intensive" courses must meet "Foundational Requirements" or FDRs. Any semblance of university administrative schemes to depression-era governmental programs is, of course, merely coincidental.

FDRs include readings "leading to mastery of an academic discipline." The Department of English and Rhetoric interprets that to mean "proficient use of the principal works of contemporary scholarship." In other words, courses must include works published by university professors as well as "traditional sources," with the balance increasingly in favor of royalties. In the first week, our imaginary first year student (let us call her Charlotte to honor our famous alum Tom Wolfe) takes in Nietzsche's *Birth of Tragedy* on Monday and Wednesday before downing *The Merchant of Venice* on Friday. "Prof" (as teachers are called by their students) reassures our panic-stricken Georgian viewing the syllabus on her new iPad that Shylock's play is "one of shorter ones." By purchasing iPads students assist Administration Officials in various tight-belting initiatives, among them, ensuring that faculty not print syllabi. Granted, I am not privy to our university's budget, but it does seem that this concession to technology kept the mulch budget intact.

FDRs serve various purposes, first and foremost engineering a "well balanced student" (to speak in administrative lingo). To her English composition course, Charlotte adds social science. She does this by clicking a box on her screen while her English professor stares into a computer screen on his lectern unable to decipher how he can project the syllabus onto the whiteboard of the newly remodeled "Smart Classroom." Charlotte is familiar with Registrar's navigation system because (at the insistence of the Under Secretary for Institutional Effectiveness) it incorporates the best features of Twitter, Facebook and Amazon.com. It is also fully integrated with social media. She gives her English course a "Like ?" even though it is early in the game. Over at "Institutional Effectiveness" the tallies and then zipped to academic deans who use the data for promotion and tenure decisions. Clearly the standards for tenure and promotion are on the rise.

Politics' reputation as the best course to fulfill a social science requirement prompts her to click on "Introduction to American Government." It drops seamlessly into her shopping cart. Introductory Politics courses do not require math, the last delinquent discipline among the social sciences. She decides to purchase her Politics texts before meeting her professor. After meandering through two floors of t-shirts, shot glasses with the university's coat of arms, and golf umbrellas, she finds a cavernous book section in a dark corner on the third floor of the bookstore. To the hundred and fifty dollar textbook she'll have to lug around campus in a backpack big enough to fit a keg, turns out that the politics prof also requires the Federalist Papers and Alexis de Tocqueville's *Democracy in America*. She is appalled by another last minute addition, Robert Penn Warren's *All the King's Men* (paper-bound copy also required). Adding insult to injury, Charlotte must also subscribe to either the *New York Times* or *Wall Street Journal* (agreeing to a tablet version is the prof's concession to technology). Inspired by IT skills he learned at the "Faculty Academy," our American Government prof assigns a daily blog post for each student to share "your rumination of the day's news." He promises to read these "with as much care as you will undoubtedly take in writing them."

FDR's clearly distinguish between the "soft" and the "hard sciences," or as we would "beverages" and "spirits." During the ten minutes her English prof needed to project the syllabus Charlotte completed her registration. To her government course she added "Introduction to Biology" (a section designed specifically for non-majors and promising no math). Back at checkout, a fellow student waiting in line with Charlotte says that their 1000 page biology textbook weighs more than a human brain. Charlotte tweets this bit of useful knowledge. While the clerk is tallying the merchandise ($995.00, which is a bit misleading if you don't subtract the Under Armour compression underwear with school logo imprint on the backside), Charlotte thumbs through her bio textbook's Table of Contents. Within the five hours campus culture parses out for each class per week, Charlotte will master the scientific method, cells, DNA, genes, ecosystems, and the inner life of a fungus.

True to the practices of ancient Greeks, Charlotte came to college to play intercollegiate athletics. A nerd she is not. Lacrosse attracts the most academically gifted students, I am told, although I continue to hear rumblings from men's rugby. Charlotte knew long ago that she would play lacrosse and only lacrosse. Her father, a native of Tennessee, renown for his organically grown and hand-picked herbal medicines, used to say half-jokingly that he would not pay for tuition should Charlotte choose another sport. Truth be told, his Colombian import-export business had not fared well during the last depression. Our collegian was weaned on her father's stories of lacrosse, a game he called "the little brother of war." The phrase harks back to his admiration of Cherokee warriors (or it may have been Iroquois, Charlotte does not remember). Native Americans invented the game as pre-war festival to entice the gods' favor before battle, so her father claimed. "Striking another player on the head and killing him is a sign of prowess," he would say in full demonstration mode holding mom's broom and growling like the monsters in *Where the*

Wild Things Are. Gestures such as these attest to the manly virtues of sport, her father said. He regaled Charlotte on the virtues of his college days before co-education. The demise of lacrosse began well before that, according to her father's genealogy. She remembers his rants at the "civilizing" effects of the French who supposedly "stole" lacrosse from Native Americans. Charlotte's father was always inclined to fair dealing and so he never missed the opportunity to thank the French for preserving the key pre-game rituals. Among various character and team-building exercises, Charlotte's father emphasized "going to water" (a story always accompanied by a wink that to this day Charlotte does not understand).

Lacrosse practices mid-afternoon rule out all classes after 2:00 p.m. Now in her adviser's office, Charlotte tells this unnamed adult that the only option left for her fourth course is "World History: 1500 - Present." She points to her iPad and he in turn learns how to find the course listed on his. The university no longer purchases desktops for faculty (another vote in favor of mulch). Charlotte looks distressed. "It starts at 9 AM and my roommate told me not to take classes before ten." Prof says that she should not worry. Evidence of her good fortune is that he's "Staff" assigned to teach it. Charlotte remains nonplussed. She might be more sympathetic had she known that the class is not fully enrolled and runs the risk of getting cancelled. Attentive to the numbers over at "institutional Effectiveness," our recently hired and untenured prof says that "World History: The Beginning to 1500" is not required (neither is he teaching it). Charlotte asks about the number of texts assigned. He speaks about the various "seminal texts on historical method" and most enthusiastically about the "central text." Charlotte is alarmed and wonders whether she can carry a load of this size. She is also concerned about the cost given her recent exploits at the bookstore. Prof hands her a 40% off coupon for a book of "contemporary literature" he says is the "central text." Faithful to his advising duties, he tells Charlotte not to purchase her books from the college bookstore. "They are gouging students. And to tell the truth, I am not pleased that they turned our bookstore into a gift shop." Charlotte catches a glimpse of the blurb on the jacket of that very book resting on the prof's lap. Something, something about "the definitive critique of the idea of major civilizations." She remembers the sign on the door and connects the author with "Staff." Just below the blurb Charlotte sees that the text is in its third edition, revised, amended, with a new introduction and much ado about "the latest developments in the field" ($49.50 after discount).

Some might say that we've imagined the "best-case scenario." If you aren't as we say these days a "traditional" student, at a four-year residential college on your parent's tab or a well-deserved scholarship, must earn your keep (by paying interest on loans we hope will keep the government solvent until profs pick up Social Security), and therefore don't have the luxury of extra-curricular activities (pre-gaming, front-loading and such), this is not a life that endears you our fictitious Charlotte. It behooves us to remain open-minded and tolerant. Were any person to put these syllabi side by side (an exercise most profs should and don't do), parse out the homework assignments each day and proceeded in earnest to complete the "work load" just as each prof deems "required," do you think our young scholar would have some difficulty carrying the work-load? Without complicating this too much by factoring in attendance (which some profs ceremoniously announce in bold on the syllabus), how much do you think she'd learn? What would she remember in the twenty hours campus culture imbibes among the student body for intellectual pursuits? And to what end? We haven't asked what use these "seminal works in the discipline" are to a banker, engineer, a manager of a restaurant, small business owner, a father and mother educating good citizens. Ask instead about the quantity and speed of consumption and what these do to Charlotte's dispositions and habits of learning. How "balanced" is she when she sits down at 10 PM to assess how much "front loading" she has to do before class the next day? Charlotte looks at her neatly typed Comic Sans "to do" list on her iPad. She has three acts from *A Comedy of Errors*, selections from Stanley Fish's *Is There a Text in This Class?* (the question is rhetorical), the chapters in Tocqueville in-between "Why the Americans are More Addicted to Practical than Theoretical Sciences" to "What Causes Most Americans to Follow Industrial Callings," for the next day and also needs to prepare the dreaded Fungus exam. Charlotte is anxious and decides to add a few apocalyptic images to her Facebook Timeline before tweeting her friends who instantaneously respond with an offer of palliatives to ease her nerves before a long night of study. If she decides in favor of her "tranquility" and takes the night to "socialize" with friends before returning to her studies after midnight, would you blame her? How fit is she for her 9 AM history course and the lacrosse double-header this coming weekend?

III

The texture and the taste of our intellectual inheritance are not as they were for the sixteenth century French aristocrat, politician, counselor to royalty, averagely endowed ladies man who speaks to us now. Appearances are deceiving. Odd as it may sound, Michel de Montaigne's Essays are as up-to-date as anything we can scroll through on the front page of the New York Times or graze on Academic.com's "cutting edge research." We are all heirs of an intellectual inheritance. Each one of us is some artifact of culture. Each one of us formed by habits of mind. Each one of us endowed with some sense of propriety and impropriety. And these imbibed by the spirit of communities we breathe and drink. This is true even of the most tolerant whose culture it is to accept all cultures promiscuously and live none consummately. In Montaigne's day there was no creative cloud to upload, no hyperlink to hyperlink surf wave after wave over the Wikipedia abyss. Yet you and I are Montaigne.

Montaigne wrote at the dawn of an encyclopedic age. His modernity was, as ours, burgeoning, fluid, and dynamic. It was (as it is now) contentious. Cultural and religious wars abounded. Mutating civilizations prompt questions. What is authoritative? What is legitimate? Who is author? What of my conscience and liberty in the face of cultural norms? Montaigne responds with humor and insight. Amidst chaos of difference, diversity, and disparity, Montaigne reconstitutes himself. Not with a treatise, a novel, a grand narrative in any traditional sense. Not quite fact and not quite fiction. He assays himself and in so doing shapes an image that reflected back is co-substantial with him. Not infelicitously has Sarah Bakewell called Montaigne the first blogger.[2]

Blogger is not as infelicitous as it may sound. Montaigne writes and reads like a drunkard. Tossed about by the opinions of authors indelibly carved into his consciousness and chosen for him, difficult to know where the tradition ends and Montaigne begins. Plato, Seneca, Lucretius inform and haunt him because he is made by them. Custom is a cruel mistress. And yet Montaigne finds himself. He bears witness to the possibility that we are more than the accretions of a fragmentary cultural inheritance ingested indiscriminately. Students often say that in the Essays they find a real person, a flesh and blood Michel de Montaigne, so very much himself, him and oddly enough also me. It is uncanny how close he is to me, they say, more "me" that "I." The "I" is always prone to self-delusion. Montaigne writes to sustain and dispel illusions, yours and mine. He does so humanely and with comic relief, prompting an occasional hearty laugh at our all-too-human frailty and stupidity. When sluggish under the burden of indiscriminate syllabi, Montaigne offers cathartic releases from time, place, and circumstance. He does so responsibly. Howsoever at odds with convention you and I are, Montaigne knows that we cannot do without. We are the stuff of laws, traditions and cultures. So how has this distant relative managed to say what I would have said of myself, me who desires to know of myself but lacks the wit, eloquence, and the

---

[2] "What We Bloggers Owe Montaigne," *The Paris Review*, November 12, 2010. Accessed July 11, 2012 @ http://www.theparisreview.org/blog/2010/11/12/what-bloggers-owe-montaigne/. See also her *How to Live: a Life of Montaigne in One Question and Twenty Attempts at an Answer* (New York: Other Press, 2010.)

courage of his simple virtues? Whence those simple virtues of his no less grand and noble for their simplicity? By what inspiration and wisdom does he depict our humanity, fragility, strength and integrity? How is he closer to us now than those dead paragons of virtue ever were, even to their contemporaries?

Jean Starobinski's *Montaigne in Motion* is a rare form of scholarly "criticism" (I doubt the term applies without qualification, but for customary reasons allow me to use it). He shares with the "Geneva School" a phenomenological reading that aims to reconstitute forms of consciousness as they are represented in literary texts. A few sentences past, I mentioned the curious marriage between "I" or "You," reader and writer. Montaigne crafts essays that draw us into an experience that is curiously as much subject (reader) as they are object (text). This is surprising, especially in the academy. Science demands an impartial objective gaze divorced from subjective preferences. Drunkenness blurs the dichotomy. It is Montaigne's metaphor for that necessary, wonderful, presumptuous and perilous movement from "self" to "other" and "other" to "self."

A prejudice enforces an inviolable subjective "I" facing static objective "things." We could trace its source to the dichotomy between "body" and "mind," but won't. Suffice to say that we appeal to the common sense distinction between ideas and experiences, thoughts and actions, theory and practice. There is truth to common sense. Sitting here with my MacBook Pro imagining Montaigne in his tower is not the same as walking up and mulling about Montaigne's tower in France. We know as much. What vexes us is the curious place or moment or event (our metaphors are inadequate) where and when mind meets body and body mind. There is more. How we see affects what we see. We train the eye. We practice the eye. And so too exercise all of our senses. We come full circle. How do we cultivate the virtues of mind so that we may live well? How may our imaginary Charlotte enjoy an intellectual education that is also a social education, and a social education that is also an intellectual education, each mutually sustaining and informing? These questions are still at a distance. So I suggest we look more closely at the bifurcation of thought and experience, theory and practice to glimpse the odd unity of fact and fiction, personal story and philosophical rumination.

A casual reader of the *Essays* is unlikely to miss Montaigne's sensitivity to body and individuality. His "To the Reader" announces Montaigne's private intent; he writes for family and about trivial affairs of no grand human scope. Only to turn that announcement on its head. Montaigne moves from the minutiae of his own experience to humanity writ large and back. We see this when Montaigne shares the intimate details of his bodily movements—or in our parlance "health." According to Starobinski Montaigne has more than titillation in mind. Of all the sciences Montaigne inherited from antiquity, Starobinski writes, medicine seems best equipped to attend to our general humanity and our particular individuality. Greek medicine "combined theory with experience, tempering one with the other." An appreciation for "unique occurrences" was not unrelated to the Greek's skepticism about appearances. In antiquity, those practiced in the art of medicine were receptive to diversity, individuality, and singularity.

Yet medicine, particularly when faithful to Galen's authority (as it was in Montaigne's day), "did not resist the temptation to erect itself into a system; it petrified and became dogma." Physicians relied, Starobinski continues, "upon a physics and physiology that hypostatized the data of sense and perception and never raised doubts about their validity." When invoking "experience," medicine men did so mostly to confirm what was already known. Rarely doubting "the substantial qualities they found in all bodies of the universe . . . they boasted of knowing the exact nature of every disease and the specific effects of every drug."[3] A distinction between disease and illness, pain and suffering may help us appreciate what is at stake in tension between claims to know experience (ideas and theories) and experience itself (practices and habits).

Two persons, call them Jack and Jill, walk through a forest together. Ticks carrying Lyme spirochetes bite both. Both "get" Lyme's disease and develop nasty co-infections, Babeosis and Bartonella among them. Within a few months, Jack and Jill are awash in fevers, chills, spikes in blood pressure, night sweats, diarrhea, insomnia, and both get lost driving in the neighborhood they once navigated without second thought. Their neurological pain is so severe that daily doses of opiates and Valium are indispensable if they are to be tolerable company among others and with themselves. Jill is tenacious, changes her diet, learns how to meditate through pain, and takes the prescribed homeopathic concoctions along with a steady stream of antibiotics. She finds a way off opiates, learns to live well and with Grace. Jack follows the same pharmacology but does slightly less than Jill to come to terms with his relationship to his own ailments. Depression takes hold and he ends up in a psyche ward. Would we ascribe the different responses to the same diseases and therapies to psychology or physiology? If both have the same disease, does it necessarily

[3] Starobinski, *Montaigne in Motion*,142.

follow that both had the same illness? Say we can measure Jack and Jill's pain "objectively." In our imaginary scale, both register 8 out of 10. Do they each experience their pain in the same way simply by virtue of having it? By our measurements of it? Does their idiosyncratic relationship to their pain alter the character or their suffering?

Jack and Jill both know Lyme. They know how it reaches into the very structure of their DNA and alters their nature. No doubt, they "experience" Lyme and a ravaged-by-it "Experience" is not an unadulterated datum of consciousness, however. Is not experience also memory mixed with imaginations, reconceptions, and dispositions, along with a host of bodily sensations? The moment we recast "experience" to ourselves, don't we abstract from *the* experience? Montaigne's subtle descriptions of and allusions to experience illumine the limits of our hard and fast dichotomies. Starobinski writes:

> As for the concept of experience, Montaigne points out that it can be used in two radically different ways. There is, first of all, the physicians' usage: based on observations that in many cases are woefully inadequate, they cite the cases they have dealt with, adduce tenuous causes, and draw misleading conclusions by making questionable analogies and comparisons and invoking infallible powers and salutary effects. Then there is the more modest attitude, Montaigne's own, which sticks to the sensible phenomena and limits itself to recording without conceptualizing; experience in this sense remains closer to what actually happens, and it would be pointless to look to it for the means to a wider knowledge along with insight into antecedent causes and ulterior consequences. We stand at the semantic dividing line that will subsequently develop into an ever-widening chasm between the "objective" experiment [expérience in French -- Trans.] of modern science, with its insistence upon sophisticated methodology, and "personal" (or

"inner") experience, wherein each individual feels the unique quality of his own existence.[4]

In Montaigne's essay "Of experience," Starobinski finds a "radical opposition between medical experience, which, having made nature the object of observation, seeks to control and thwart nature's operations, and *contemplative* personal experience, which resigns itself to ignorance of nature's operations and submits to taking nature for a guide, solely in the hope of leading a wiser life and suffering a less contorted death"[5] (emphases mine).

Of education, students say "intellectual" and "social." Academicians say "theory" and "practice." Both separate what is "thought" from what is "done." Responding to the ills of mind-body dualism, we turn every human act into physiology and then to mechanism. True, thoughts have a physiology, as do deeds. If Starobinski is correct, the movement in Montaigne is not from mind-body dualism to mind-body monism. Montaigne offers a contemplative third that seems to hover over mind-body while remaining tethered to mind-body. Athletes learn technique. They train arduously, rigorously, and according to a logical plan. On race day that technique has to be "forgotten." It also has to be "remembered" by the body as "natural" movement. Spectators are aware of the differences between an athlete in the "zone" and one in his or her "head." Athletes in the "flow" are at ease, their motions fluid, seemingly effortless. Technique becomes second nature. Athletes in the midst of competition worrying about their technique look unhappy and are unsuccessful. They look engineered. Cham-

[4] Starobinski, *Montaigne in Motion*,142-43.
[5] Ibid.,145.

pions do not forgo technique. They do not train absent reason, logic, and calculation. Nor are they unaware howsoever submerged that technique needed to be for them to perform naturally.

IV.

"Lets get back to our bottles." Reader, imagine you've experienced a few glassfuls of wine. If not, grab a bottle and come back to this essay. Pour yourself a tall one. I won't do as Roger Scruton and ask for your knowledge of wine. Imagine your palate is as uneducated as mine. Smell. Take a sip. Don't swallow. Taste. Swallow and then another sip… close your eyes. How does wine travel from mouth, to throat, to cheeks and fingertips. And beyond. Imagine you are in good company, good enough to lose yourself a bit. I won't ask how many glasses that usually takes. Some of you require more than a bottle (or two) to be somehow other than (or is it more fully?) yourself. Don't try to compete with my imaginary research assistant. He's a star. Drink enough so that the ugliest person in the room looks attractive. If your friends look like mine, you're past the point of no return. *Contemplate* a state of consciousness where the edges of your boundaries fade. Allow the edges of persons and things to fade also. Time is neither here nor there. Space is neither yesterday nor tomorrow.

Montaigne's *Essays* are paths into contemplative consciousness, not the expected academic explications of contemplative consciousness. Labyrinthine by design, they thwart our customary strategies of interpretation. His juxtapositions are so arresting, even jarring at times, that we must pause, think, wonder how I got from here to there. Critical thinking alone will not do. Critical thinking alone may frustrate more than it assists our reading. References to authors and historical figures abound. While they certainly put Montaigne's erudition on display, his purposes are not merely vain. Michel invites us to wonder: Who is the narrator of these *Essays*? Quotes lifted from who knows where are strung together incessantly. Any reader would be excused if he or she were to wonder if it is Montaigne who speaks, if he or she is reading Montaigne's interpretation of an author or his interpretation of an interpretation of an interpretation of someone who supposedly said something but is now dead. Classical author after classical author paraphrased, misquoted, quoted out of context and with no suggested context at all. If not history, then what are the *Essays*—biography? To be sure, Montaigne shares intimate details of his own life. More than we need to know (but seem unable to do without), including the machinations, lies, and infidelities of his father. Readers are guilty of their own reading of Montaigne. Some go on to become co-conspirators in the crime of writing. Montaigne's *Essays* are galleries, movies projected on the walls of our mind's cave. Stories replete with political intrigue and innuendo. He paints with metaphor and allegory. With Montaigne we are dreamy. Some of what Montaigne says of medicine seems preposterous, or to put it bluntly (as you may already have), call them a rant. Until we shed our presumption and carefully consider how he says what he says and to what end, all we see, and hear, and feel is our indignation. That too turns us into accomplices. Neuroscientists will someday send readers of Montaigne's *Essays* through an fMRI. Then we'll believe because there is data showing the effects of contemplative reading and writing. In our not-too-distant present neuroscientists will demonstrate that there is a physiology to Montaigne contemplatively read no less fascinating than Buddhist monks in meditative states.

Drunkenness is a metaphor and Montaigne was not the first to resort to it as an image of philosophy. That contemplation is of the nature of philosophy has better spokespersons than me.[6] Plato before him and Friedrich Nietzsche after him are two of his better-known accomplices. Philosophy and philosophers are caricatured as rationalists. Right so, I suppose, for mind is some part *ratio*. Mind is also imagination and feeling and sensation and intuition. We in the academy who supposedly live the "life of the mind" would have to exercise mind beyond our narrowly circumscribed "critical thinking" to be true to our vocation. Our students should be taught how to be wholly themselves (that is, wholly human) through their encounter with good books. And for this they need stories of real human beings with a pulse, characters who care, love, hope, fear, err, fail, who are angry and inspired and discover that they are somehow more and less than they imagine themselves to be. Does transcendence lead to excess? Sure. We've been warned. On the Sixth Day the Lord God created human and Lord God saw that human exceeded the good. That is what "very good" means. The reckless intoxication of our students is a spiritual malady borne of a constriction of mind that demands a rebellion of soul.

I am not going to leave you with hypocritical hand wringing. My appeal is for a contemplative rhetoric and style and draws us back to the likes of Montaigne not to say what

[6] Josef Pieper, *Happiness and Contemplation*, Introduced by Ralph McInerny, Translated by Richard and Clara Winston (South Bend, IN: St. Augustine's Press, 1998).

they are about but instead to be with them. This is not to counsel vice. Let Roger Scruton speak for me:

> For if society is sometimes threatened by intoxicants, it is equally threatened by the lack of them. Without their aid we see each other as we are, and no human society can be built on so frail a foundation. The world is besieged by destructive illusions, and recent history has made us wary of them, so wary that we forget that illusions are sometimes beneficial. Where would we be without the belief that human beings can face down disaster and swear undying love? But such a belief persists only if renewed in imagination, and how can this occur if we have no escape route from the evidence?[7]

In the place of sanctimonious discourse on the vices of student "social life," I leave you with some suggestive hints that may provide evidence for a contemplative reading of Montaigne. Be mindful that these are hints, illustrations if you are a charitable reader, a suggestive reading "Of Drunkenness" that may justify the embellishments foreshadowed. Less am I persuaded that readers of this essay need a guide than I of my inability to offer it. An explanation is not contemplation. Data from an fMRI may chart the course of a monk's meditating brain. That is not the same as mediation itself.

"Of Drunkenness" echoes one of Montaigne's most cited essays, "That to philosophize is to learn to die." It calls us back to Socrates. The context is melancholic. "The world is nothing but variety and dissimilarity" (II:2,244).[8] If there is lament, it is quickly turned over to the Stoics. "Vices are all alike in that

---

[7] Roger Scruton, *I Drink Therefore I am: A Philosopher's Guide to Wine* (New York: Continuum, 2012) 1.

[8] *The Complete Essays of Montaigne*, Translated by Donald Frame (Stanford, CA: Stanford University Press, 1965). Citation includes volume, essay, and page numbers. Hereinafter cited by page number only.

they are all vices, and perhaps this is the way the Stoics understand it" (II:2,244). Perhaps. Humans are prone to vice. No life is unblemished. That said, we cannot leave the question of how to live well to this abstract consideration of "vice." Montaigne continues: "But although they are equally vices, they are not equal vices" (II:2,244). All vices partake of vice. However, infidelity is not vicious in say watching HBO's "Game of Thrones" is vicious. Which begs a question. Which is the better vice? "Confusion about the order and measurement of sins is dangerous" (II:2,244). Much to ponder in the shift from vice to sin. I leave the reader to him or herself. "Murderers, traitors, tyrants, gain to much by it," that is, by the relative discrimination of vices. Or by the absence of discrimination among different souls: "It is not right that their conscience should be relieved because some other man is indolent, or lascivious, or less assiduous in his devotions" (II:2,244-45). We find easy expiation of our sins by estimating the disgrace of others more highly than our own. "Each man lays weight on his neighbor's sin and lightens his own" (II:2,245). Charlatans are among the teaching profession too. "Even teachers often weigh sins badly, in my opinion" (II:2,245). Do not disregard "opinion." A world of variety and dissimilarity is confounded more deeply by disparate and competing opinions. Words confuse things.

Socrates' introduction is timely. Such is the task of the philosopher to illumine the cave of opinion. "As Socrates used to say…the principal function of wisdom was to distinguish good things from bad" (II:2,244). The philosopher's art if necessary for us "lesser men, who even at our best are always tainted with vice" (II:2,245). We, however, are not versed in wisdom. We should say "the same thing about the *science* of distinguishing among vices" (emphasis mine). And that is: "if we do not make this distinction very nicely, the virtuous man and the wicked man will remain confused and unrecognized." All men look alike, the wicked no different from the virtuous. Nor does our mediocrity and viciousness prevent us from speaking (and we are speaking about speaking) to the distinction between virtue and sin. Montaigne does as our academic abstracts do, announce what is to come. A variety of opinions in a deceptive world of appearances and similitude is some important part of his thesis. At this junction, Montaigne turns disoriented readers to topic as entitled. From drunken minds we turn to drunken bodies.

Montaigne tells lavish stories of drunkards and shares your incredulity. "I should not have believed in drunkenness so seep, so dead and buried, if I had not read of this instance of it in the histories" (II:2,246). This prompts him to ponder the various drinking styles of Germans and French I noted earlier. Out of nowhere, he follows up with an incredible story of his own. "It is marvelous," Montaigne writes, "what stories I have heard my father tell of his chastity" (II:2,247). We read that Dad was just the man to tell such stories "being well suited to the service of the ladies, by nature and art" (II:2,247). This is marvelous, so Montaigne suggests, his father so poorly constituted for fidelity yet so gifted by nature and practiced by art. R. W. Emerson wrote of Montaigne: "The sincerity and marrow of the man reaches to his sentences. I know not any where a book that seems less written. It is the language of conversation transferred to a book. Cut these words, and they would bleed; they are vascular and alive."[9] Emerson had a sense of humor.

[9] R.W. Emerson, "Montaigne; or, the Skeptic."

Let us stay here, just with this storied interlude. Montaigne's story-telling dad is said to be curiously Laconic. That would be in keeping with the essay's beginning. Stoics are men of few words, occupied as they undoubtedly are with the action. Although, as Montaigne's frequent use of their words implies, one secretly wishes they were as restrained in word as they were virtuous in deed. Telling stories of his story-telling dad, Montaigne says that his father "spoke little and well, and sprinkled his language with ornamental expressions from books in the modern vernaculars, especially Spanish" (II:2,247-48). Is this Montaigne or Montaigne's dad? I am not going to speculate how Spanish is supposed to assist us when our purpose is to tell prodigious lies in French to a household whose members had for several years of the young Montaigne's life been admonished to speak only Latin. Note in passing, and the hint will suffice, that Montaigne's mother Antoinette de Louppes de Villanueva was of Spanish and Jewish descent. Montaigne's ancestors were persecuted by the Inquisition and persuaded to convert to Catholicism—I suspect the earlier indictment referred to sins not vices. Antoinette is to be commended. Montaigne was born to a lineage of expatriates who held on to their Jewish faith (mind) along with impeccable Catholic observances (body). The distinction between appearance and reality should not be condemned so hastily. Montaigne does as we all do, we exploit it.

Montaigne's father knew how to conceal his words no less prodigiously than his deeds. Although speaking little, he spoke wisely. Dad "sprinkled his language with ornamental expressions from books in the modern vernaculars" (II:2,247-48). Coincidentally, Spanish was the modern vernacular his father preferred. Has Montaigne impregnated his French essays with Latin seed? One book in particular appealed to Montaigne's father, the one "they call Marcus Aurelius" (II:2,248). Montaigne gives the author's name, not the title. A footnote in the Donald Frame edition directs us the reader to "The Golden Book of Marcus Aurelius, by Antonio de Guevara (1490-1545), a historical romance popular in France, Italy, and England as well as Spain" (II:2,248). Frame is mischievous and thankfully says nothing more. Antonio de Guevara is not your household name. If he is, drink some more. The name Montaigne gives (not the book title) makes us think of Marcus Aurelius, Emperor of Rome (A. D. 161-180), and author of his own *Meditations*. Remember, the essay starts with a meditation on the Stoics. And now we are at Marcus Aurelius. But the reference is to a Spanish version or a translation. In Spanish, translator is "traductor," a word derived from "triador" meaning traitor. The etymology serves Italian and Latin too.

We read ahead in search of reasons why the name of this imperial Stoic philosopher appears through the veil (Marcus Aurelius conspicuously absent in the *Essays*). What follows is not all that helpful. Not at first blush, anyway. Immediately following the allusion to the life of the Stoic philosopher Marcus Aurelius (who, by the way, wrote his meditations in Greek not Latin), Montaigne offers a description of his father that lavishly praises ends up praising the propriety and moderation of the stoics. Yes, the Stoics. Such good dinner guests aren't they? "Honey, If you want to invite Cato, go ahead and invite Cato. Just make sure he stays clear of the steak knives. And remember, Socrates always wants the Hemlock in a large pewter Stein." To his father's moderated and ornamental language, Montaigne notes his moderate features. His father's bearing, we learn, "was one of gentle, humble and very modest gravity" (II:2,248). Montaigne describes him scrupulously dressed, endowed with well-proportioned features, a manly and conscientious character. A perfect gentleman, we could say.

This ordinary man appears supernaturally endowed. Montaigne says that his father "has left some small miracles in people's memory" (II:2,248). Montaigne's father had a fitness regime that would put Matthew McConaughey and Cameron Diaz to shame. Maybe these actors date me. Let us try a couple of "Twilight" idols instead: Taylor Lautner and... Does Kristen Stewart workout? How about Katniss Everdeen? Montaigne did not witness to his father's supernatural accomplishments. He knows only from hearsay. The young scholar remembers "some canes filled with lead, with which they say he exercised his arms to prepare for throwing the bar or the stone, or for fencing, and some shoes with leaded soles to train him to be lighter in running and jumping" (11:2,248). But then it's not all hearsay. "I have seen him, past sixty, put our agility to shame: leap into the saddle in his furred gown, do a turn over the table on his thumb, hardly ever go to his room without taking three or four steps at a time" (II:2,248). The distinction between hearsay and seeing with ones own eyes allows us to consider the distinction between a disciplined athlete dedicated to a training regimen that transforms ordinary movements and daily bodily tasks into artistry and habit, and those not so dedicated who take the excellence of those ordinary tasks as a supernatural gift. We also glimpse what every athlete knows, which is that when you are in the zone you are not "thinking" about techniques. The moment you start thinking about techniques, you're not performing. We learn forgetting. Action requires conscious forgetting or unconscious remembering. So does reading.

How many places do we travel in one paragraph in "Of drunkenness?" The movement throughout is not as disjointed as it seems once contemplate through a veil. Consider a possible analogy between Montaigne's father's leaps, "three or four steps at a time," and Montaigne's own prodigious feats as a writer. "On this subject of mine," these are the words that follow "three or four steps at a time," Montaigne would have us believe that his father, yes his father, for Montaigne's words are "On this subject of mine, he used to say," his father used to say that "in a whole province there was scarcely one woman of quality who had a bad reputation." How do we know of his father's good reputation, or, to say it as Montaigne does, the absence of his father's bad reputation? Montaigne's father "would tell of remarkable intimacies, especially his own, with respectable women, free of any suspicion. And of himself he solemnly swore that he had come to his marriage a virgin" (II:2,248).

Amazing, isn't it? That a man so seemingly ordinary, not so extraordinarily endowed by nature, yet who does not curse Nature's stinginess and instead takes it as encouragement to perfect a clandestine artistry and ingenuity that to the ordinary observer appears like extraordinary spectacle graced by the gods, this ordinary man enjoys frequent intimacies with "respectable women" themselves able to stay "free of any suspicion." All of which allow Montaigne's father to marry a virgin. The story ends with another wonder. Montaigne writes of his father's excursions:

> And yet he had taken a very long part in the Italian wars, of which he has left a diary in his own hand, following what happened point by point, in both public and private matters. Consequently he married well along in age, in the year 1528,

which was his thirty-third, on his return from Italy. Let's get back to our bottles. (II:2,248)

Marcus Aurelius wrote his *Meditations* in preparation for and during military campaigns. War is brutal. It turns our virtues into vices and vices into virtues. Successful prosecution of strategies requires less than the truth. Publics are kept in the dark, misled when their preservation requires is. Military leaders must adapt to changing circumstances—contingency, surprise, accident, error, unintended consequences, the fickle, greedy, rapacious nature of some men, friends too. Where is virtue amidst mayhem and the omnipresence of death? Let this question belong to you, not me.

V.

Drunkenness is Montaigne's metaphor for that loosening of self that makes us tolerable to ourselves and open to the individuality of another. Individuality and difference should be protected and celebrated. We should pause before speaking of "man" and "human nature." Let us be wary of mushy sentimentality that dissolves us quickly into the "One." Tyranny is made of such stuff. A world of reified "subjects" and "objects" will not do, however. Such a "world" betrays the stuff that a good life is made of: love, friendship, community, and spirit. Howsoever self-made we assume we are, we don't rid ourselves of the longing for a "university" in a "universe." Please, some vision and purpose to unite us not perpetually divide us.

The prospects of a Montaigne that lives in us, inspires, educates, edifies, chastens, and, dare I say, may even guide, requires teachers. Montaigne well read is Montaigne well taught. Alone Montaigne's *Essays* will not become today's bestseller. He won't accompany our students headed to the beach for a summer vacation. Montaigne's rhetoric is deliberately discombobulating. Students greet the first pages of the *Essays* with delight and consternation. What? Why this? Did he really say what I think he said? He was not just talking about his unruly member, was he? Mom and dad call: "Honey, tell me what you're studying that political philosophy course of yours?" No need to even mention what our colleagues over in analytical philosophy or the real social sciences think of "essays." Montaigne knew of presumptions and prejudices like these. Innovations of Montaigne's kind are not the stuff "leadership studies." Creative souls are freaks—often vilified, ostracized, censored, ignored, imprisoned, and these failing, killed. Words matter. They reach deep into the genome of the soul. Such knowledge is simultaneously revelatory, of what was, and is, and regenerative, of what could be. Life is not a theory.

That's a lot to put on Montaigne's shoulders: past, present, and future, the bridge between I and other, subject and object, body and soul. Such experiences do not lend themselves readily to proof. Experiences do lend themselves to intelligibility. Life is through and through mind. And that is our task—mindfulness. Words lend intelligibility to experience. At first glance the phrase "intelligibility of experience" looks like one of those self-evident truths, some part of common sense. There lies the rub. Common sense is both "common," that is, shared by or constitutive of all, and "sense," that is, of feeling not of mind. Its just "there." We either have it or we don't. But does the matter rest there? Do we not educate the senses? A song streaming through on Spotify or Pandora and I say to my guitar-playing son, do you hear the riff? An art teacher says to my paintbrush happy daughter looking at a Monet hanging on a wall at the National Gallery, can you imagine the stroke? Is the "common" not flexible? Wearing a cap in class would outrage my father; it only mildly disturbs today's profs. Why do students resort to "like" each time a phrase reaches a natural pause? Language, art, sensibilities are tutored and we are not always conscious of the transformations. Montaigne writes essays that seem to be about "nothing." They are oddly enough about everything.

In contemporary parlance, the relationship between act and imagination is called "mind-body." That we are in the midst of a "mind-body" revolution is undeniable. Scroll through the pages of *The New York Times* or *The Guardian* and search for "mindfulness," "contemplation," "neuroplasticity," and the "like." The Association for Contemplative Mind in Higher Education (ACMHE) was born in 2008, conceived by "hard core" scientists inspired the demonstrable effects of meditation. Neuroscientists, humanist scholars, and Buddhist monks collaborate in the search for a description of mind that unites first and third person perspectives. Courses in contemplative business, political science, sociology, abound throughout the academy. Within a few years every university discipline will have some contemplative component. In the spring of 2012 the first ever International Symposium for Contemplative Studies met in Denver, Colorado, a motley crew of doctors, clinicians, K-12 teachers, social workers and social scientists reaching for ways of thinking, doing, and being that do more than reduce us to "critical thinkers" or "rational thinkers" in the economy of "all against all."

To recover a bit of history in the genealogy of the neurosciences before they became real sciences is not the principal reason for reading Montaigne. The present danger is that all disciplines will soon be subsumed under the umbrella of the neurosciences. The explanatory power of the neurosciences is not the concern. By all means, all who care for the so-called "life of the mind" come to terms with the neurosciences. Montaigne is important because he writes before the rhetoric of science conquered the language we now use for mind-body disciplines. He is a neuro-rhetorician before we found the need for a new term. That he thinks through the rhetoric of self-awareness and gives expression to it in ways that make us self-aware attests to an experience of mind-body that is independent of the rhetoric of science. Doing so preserves the independence, nay the very possibility of philosophy. Without the preserve of philosophy, knowledge of the self is nothing more than self-help gobbledygook. We are left with what scientists disparagingly call "stories" and no way of discriminating between them. Including the story of science. Then all we may really know of ourselves is what an fMRI printout "tells" the interpreter. An fMRI reading and self-knowledge are not incompatible. Neither are they identical.

5

Eschatological Dissatisfaction: Montaigne's Response to Machiavelli on Fortune and Death

Kevin S. Honeycutt

> You see, I'm haunted by certain questions, and perhaps you'll allow me to ask them.
> —Dostoyevsky, *Notes from Underground*

The ancient characterization of philosophy as the human response to mortality is best given in Plato's *Phaedo,* where Socrates says that those who philosophize rightly are practicing to die (*hoi orthos philosophountes apothneskein meletosi*; 64a). The modern counterpart to this characterization is Montaigne's essay, "That to philosophize is to learn to die" (*Que philosopher c'est apprendre à mourir*).[1] Though Montaigne in his *Essays*

[1] All parenthetical citations of Montaigne are given by book number, essay number, and page number (e.g., II:11,306) and are from Donald M. Frame's translation of the *Essays* (Stanford: Stanford University Press, 1943), although I have also consulted M.A. Screech's translation (London: Penguin Books, 1991). For the most part, Frame follows the Bordeaux Copy, which is a copy of the 1588 (5th) edition. See the French edition by Pierre Villey and V.L. Saulnier, 3 vols., 2nd edition (Paris: Presses Universitaires de France, "Quadrige," 1992). Concerning the addition of the 1595 material and the status of the manuscript tradition, see Frame's introduction to his translation, xv. Montaigne insists upon the unity of the various editions: "I add, but I do not correct…My book is always one" (*tousjours un*; III:9,736).

claims that he is a "new figure: an unpremeditated and accidental philosopher" (II:12,409), he is thus to some extent in the Platonic tradition.[2] Plato and Montaigne both make death a central concern of philosophy and thus stand together as defenders of a certain understanding of the task of the philosopher.

The figure that stands most apart from this characterization of philosophy is Machiavelli.[3] In his *Discourses on Livy*, he says that he "seek[s] unknown waters and lands" and "take[s] a path as yet untrodden by anyone."[4] In his *Prince*, he departs from the customary manner of advising princes (DL.3-4); he derides those who have imagined republics and principalities that have never been seen in truth, suggesting that he will focus instead on what men actually do (15.61). If there is anyone famous for imagining a republic, it is Plato, and thus Machiavelli's remarks appear to distance his thought from that of Plato. But there is a subtlety here not to be overlooked, with the result that perhaps

---

[2] Compare Ann Hartle, *Michel de Montaigne: Accidental Philosopher* (Cambridge: Cambridge University Press, 2003) 3

[3] All parenthetical citations of Machiavelli are given by chapter number and page number (e.g., 6.21) and are from the second edition of Harvey C. Mansfield's translation of *The Prince* (Chicago: University of Chicago Press, 1998) although I have also consulted Mark Musa's bilingual edition (New York: St. Martin's Press, 1964). With minor emendations, Mansfield and Musa both follow the 1929 manuscript of Mario Casella. See *Tutte le opere*, ed. Mario Casella and Guido Mazzoni (Florence: G.Barbera, 1969). There is no original manuscript of *The Prince* in Machiavelli's hand; concerning the resulting philological disagreement over the various critical editions of *The Prince*, see A.E. Quaglio, "Per il testo 'De Principatibus' di Niccolo Machiavelli," *Lettere Italiane* 19 (1967): 141-186.

[4] From the Preface to the First Book. See *Discourses on Livy*, trans. Harvey C. Mansfield and Nathan Tarcov (Chicago: University of Chicago Press, 1996) 5.

Machiavelli is not as far from Plato's conception of philosophy as we might believe at first glance. For if there is anything that one would notice from a close inspection of what men actually do, it is that all of them die.

In what follows, I explore Machiavelli and Montaigne on fortune and death and suggest that Montaigne is directly engaging Machiavelli—a claim that requires no little defense, as Machiavelli is mentioned by name only twice in the *Essays*, and both times it is almost in passing.[5] As I will show, however, Montaigne's *Essays* touch the heart of the Machiavellian position, despite appearances to the contrary. What is the appropriate role that fortune should play in our lives and our deaths? That is the question of this essay.

Machiavelli and the Phenomenology of Deception

In order to see how Montaigne responds to Machiavelli, it would be helpful to first set forth Machiavelli's philosophical

[5] In "On presumption," Montaigne notes that Machiavelli's arguments were "solid enough for the subject" but very easy to combat (II.17.497). In "Observations on Julius Caesar's methods of making war," Montaigne notes that it is reported that many great leaders in war held certain books in particular esteem, and it is said "in our day" that Machiavelli is still in repute in other countries (II.34.556). It is worth noting that Montaigne omits any mention of Machiavelli in the essay, "Of Books," conspicuously so on at least two occasions. Montaigne notes his preference for the genre of historical biography, effusively praising the work of Plutarch ("in every way Plutarch is my man") and Diogenes Laertius ("I am very sorry that we do not have a dozen Laertiuses"). He does not mention in this context Machiavelli's *Life of Castruccio Castracani* (II.10.303). Secondly, and perhaps more tellingly, Montaigne praises the historical work of Machiavelli's friend, Guicciardini, even going so far as to transcribe the comments he made in his edition of "my Guicciardini." He does not mention in this context Machiavelli's *Florentine Histories* (II.10.305).

position as it is found in *The Prince*, since Machiavelli says that work contains "all that I have learned and understood" (*tutto quello che io ho conosciuto e inteso*; DL.3-4).[6]

The word "philosophy" never occurs in *The Prince*, and the word "philosopher" occurs only a single time (*filosofo*; 19.75). It is an epithet applied to Marcus Aurelius, one of two Roman emperors in a list of ten who did not come to a "bad end" (*tristo fine*; 19.77-78). Machiavelli admits that Marcus lived and died most honorably and that he avoided hatred from his people and contempt from his soldiers. One might think, then, that the life of Marcus would be praiseworthy—for when a prince avoids the things that generate hatred and contempt, "he

---

[6] Although it is currently customary to explicate Machiavelli's thought in terms of the *Discourses on Livy*, this remark by Machiavelli suggests that the core of his thought, if perhaps imperfectly, is contained in *The Prince*. Compare Mansfield and Tarcov, *Discourses on Livy*, 3. See also Machiavelli's letter to Francesco Vettori of 10 December 1513, where Machiavelli claims that, in *The Prince*, he delves as deeply as he can into his subject. Mansfield has included this letter in the second edition of his translation (107–11) but see also *Machiavelli: The Chief Works and Others*, vol. 2, trans. Allan Gilbert (Durham: Duke University Press, 1965) 927–31. In *Beyond Good and Evil* §28, Nietzsche suggests that the concision and pacing of *The Prince* does not detract from its depth and in fact may even add to it: "But how could the German language—even the prose of a Lessing—imitate Machiavelli's tempo—Machiavelli, who in his *Principe*, lets us breathe the fine, dry air of Florence? He cannot help presenting the most serious concerns in a boisterous *allegrissimo*, and is, perhaps, not without a malicious, artistic sense for the contrast he is risking: thoughts that are long, hard, thorough, and dangerous, and a galloping tempo and the very best and most mischievous mood." See Nietzsche, *Beyond Good and Evil*, trans. Judith Norman (Cambridge: Cambridge University Press, 1992) 29-30. See also Harvey C. Mansfield, *Machiavelli's Virtue* (Chicago: University of Chicago Press, 1998) 225; and Leo Strauss, *Thoughts on Machiavelli* (Chicago: University of Chicago Press, 1958) 16-17: "The *Prince* is as comprehensive as the *Discourses*: each book contains everything that Machiavelli knows."

will have done his part and will find no danger in his other infamies" (19.72). But Marcus was also a hereditary prince—that is, he inherited his principality—and Machiavelli says that the maintenance of a hereditary principality requires only a prince of "ordinary industry" unless there is a conflict with an extraordinary and excessive force (2.6-7). By contrast, the other survivor in the list of ten emperors is Septimius Severus, who was a new prince and who as a result may be more illustrative of the extraordinary and the excessive.[7]

The contrast between Marcus and Severus highlights two of the key themes of *The Prince*. The first is the distinction between "virtue" (*virtù*) and "fortune" (*fortuna*)—or, as Machiavelli also characterizes these terms, the reliance upon "one's own [arms]" and the "arms of others," respectively (1.6).[8] This first theme concerns the activity of a new prince; it concerns the founding or acquisition of new principalities, for "truly it is a very natural and ordinary thing to desire to acquire" (3.14). The second theme concerns the maintenance of principalities—what one might call the problem of persistence and change. It concerns how a prince can make a principality lasting when the nature of peoples (6.24), worldly

---

[7] As Mansfield notes (77n16), Severus is called a criminal at *Discourses on Livy* I.10. See Mansfield and Tarcov, *Discourses on Livy*, 32. Severus made the taking of the Eucharist a crime in Rome, as Michael Palmer notes in his *Masters and Slaves: Revisioned Essays in Political Philosophy* (Lexington: Lexington Books, 2001) 87. Montaigne speaks of "the Emperor Severus" only a single time in the *Essays* (I.36.167) although it is not clear which of the three possible emperors he means. It is Nero and not Severus that Montaigne calls "that living image of cruelty" (II.1.239).

[8] For more on Machiavelli's understanding of "virtue," see Mansfield, *Machiavelli's Virtue*, 6-52. See also Angelo M. Codevilla's introduction to his translation of *The Prince* (New Haven: Yale University Press, 1997) xix-xxxviii.

things (10.44), things in general (18.70), and even "the good" (25.100) are all, as Machiavelli tells us, "variable" (from *variare*); and when fortune is not only variable (25.101), but volatile and unstable (7.26) like the winds (18.70).

These two themes emerge early in the text, in the Dedicatory Letter, as what Machiavelli calls "threads" (*orditi*). Machiavelli's choice of *orditi* suggests that these are lengthwise threads, i.e., the warp, rather than crosswise ones, i.e., the woof or *tessuti*. The implication of his terminology is that, among others, these two themes—acquiring a principality and making it lasting—run throughout the course of the book.

In *Prince* 25, the penultimate chapter, these *orditi* reach a sort of resolution. Machiavelli says that men become unhappy when their modes become in discord with fortune—when fortune has varied and yet men have remained obstinate in their modes (25.101). As a result, if one wants to be happy, it is better to be impetuous than cautious. We are not told whether the impetuous man knows how to be cautious; however, we are told that the cautious man does not know how to be impetuous, does not know how to change either his natural inclination or his habit of walking on only one path (25.100). The cautious man, in other words, does not know how to be flexible. *Prince* 25 is something of a culmination of Machiavelli's teaching; it is where Machiavelli puts the finishing touches on his new account of virtue, one that is characterized not by moral excellence but rather by an accommodation to variability. In a rejection of the Platonic-Aristotelian position, Machiavelli frames virtue—and, indeed, happiness—not in terms of participation in a great chain of being but rather in terms of adaptation to a world of ceaseless becoming.

But this is not the only critical result of *Prince* 25. Near the beginning of the chapter, Machiavelli likens fortune to "one of these violent rivers [*uno di questi fiumi rovinosi*]" which, when enraged, will flood plains and uproot everything in its path.[9] He then elaborates this likeness with a statement about fortune's nature: fortune *is* a woman (*la fortuna è donna*). Since she is a woman—and since she will uproot everything in her rage—Machiavelli says that it is necessary, if one wants to hold her down, to beat her and strike her down (25.101).

This passage is one of the most notorious ones in *The Prince*. Leaving aside the harshness or even misogyny of such a remark,[10] one might say that the most immediate problem with it on Machiavelli's own account is that it seems to conflict with the characterization of virtue as flexibility. In other words, the precept concerning the treatment of fortune does not appear to be rooted in flexibility at all but rather in something decidedly inflexible, i.e., necessity. However, virtue is also characterized in *Prince* 25 as the ability to resist fortune (25.98). So the deeper point to be made here is that the required flexibility is inherent in the nature of virtue itself. For Machiavelli, virtue is a moral and intellectual flexibility that allows one to act in accordance with necessity without the need for any justification from the vantage point of customary morality. In other words, Machiavelli's teaching is an attempt to reduce the need to be flexible in the long run. An initial act of moral flexibility—of

---

[9] See Roger D. Masters, *Fortune is a River: Leonardo da Vinci and Niccolò Machiavelli's Magnificent Dream to Change the Course of Florentine History* (New York: Plume, 1999). Masters's title, perhaps intentionally, alters Machiavelli's words from a likeness to an identity.

[10] See Hanna Fenichel Pitkin, *Fortune is a Woman: Gender and Politics in the Thought of Niccolò Machiavelli* (Chicago: University of Chicago Press, 1999), especially chapters 5 and 6.

what from the perspective of customary morality can only be called cruelty—is required when dealing with fortune; once she is held down, it is not clear that she will have much say in the matter, and it is not clear that we will as a result have to accommodate ourselves to her afterwards.[11]

This reconfiguration of virtue has significant implications for Machiavelli's teaching, particularly his teaching on what kind of life a prince should lead. Machiavelli claims that we almost always imitate the paths beaten by others (6.22). Furthermore, he claims that we should imitate not merely anyone but rather the greatest or most excellent of such men (6.22): those who have founded new principalities by virtue, i.e., their own arms; and who have demonstrated this virtue, as we learn later, in refusing to allow fortune to demonstrate hers (25.98). But here it is important to remember the second theme of persistence and change, for there is a significant difference between founding (or acquiring) and maintaining; these are distinct activities that require distinct sets of skills. Maintenance requires foreseeing dangers, and it is not always the case that a prince who can establish a new principality, even though his own virtue, is a prince who can maintain it.

Machiavelli says that "he who does not recognize evils when they arise in a principality is not truly wise" and that this ability is "given to few" (13.57). These evils—or what Machiavelli calls "the poison that lies underneath"—can erupt at any time

[11] It is worth noting that this interpretation has the merit of making sense of other, similar textual oddities—such as a prince who needs to be flexible being offered by Machiavelli a mode that never fails (22.93) and a general rule that never fails (23.95). Machiavelli ends chapter 3 by claiming that "one may draw" from the previous discussion a rule that never or rarely fails; however, he does not do so in his own name (3.16).

from beneath the tranquility of a seemingly ordered principality, and they will ruin even virtuous principalities such as the Roman Empire (13.57). The example of Rome is particularly poignant since Machiavelli tells us earlier, in chapter 3, that the Romans are the model for all wise princes in that they have regard not only for present troubles but also for future ones (3.12). Furthermore, Machiavelli mentions the disease of consumption in both passages, drawing our attention to the comparison and suggesting that something has gone awry in Rome. What is the difference between "the Romans" (i.e., the Roman Republic) of chapter 3 and "the Roman Empire" of chapter 13? The lesson seems to be that virtue, as the ability to resist fortune, has somehow been lost or forgotten; success has dulled the sharpness of the Roman mind. As Machiavelli puts the point in a chapter entitled "Why the Princes of Italy Have Lost Their States," it is a "common defect of men not to take account of the storm during the calm" (21.94).

Part of the solution to the problem of preserving your principality is never to fall into the belief that you can find someone to pick you up when times are bad (21.97). The more important teaching, however, is never to forget that all other men are potentially dangerous to you, that you are always surrounded by the storm. "One can say this," Machiavelli says, "generally of men: that they are ungrateful, fickle, pretenders and dissemblers, evaders of danger, eager for gain" (17.66). It is perhaps fortunate, and at any rate convenient, that the solution to the problem of maintenance lies within this same generality that makes human beings dangerous to a prince in the first place. "Men in general," Machiavelli says, "judge more by their eyes than by their hands, because seeing is given to everyone, touching to a few. Everyone sees how you appear, few touch what you are..." (18.71).

This is an echo of the famous claim in chapter 15 that Machiavelli calls the "effectual truth" (*verità effettuale*; 15.61). One might call it proto-phenomenological, and indeed Kenneth Blanchard has described it as a "dramatic contraction of the horizon of philosophy."[12] It is important to be clear here as to what Machiavelli means, especially with respect to what he is rejecting. The thesis of effectual truth is not that there is no truth; in fact, Machiavelli explicitly claims that he is leaving out what is imagined and discussing what is true (15.61). The claim is rather that the truth is not what it seems according to what Machiavelli calls "the orders of others"; the truth is not something larger, as it is for Plato or Aristotle, than any human perspective and toward which all perspectives tend (or should ideally tend). The "effect" of Machiavelli's effectual truth is always the effect on some observer.[13] Milan is a wholly new principality *to* Francesco Sforza (1.5); the kingdom of Naples was partly new *to* the king of Spain (1.5); one is not permitted to call Agathocles' crimes "virtues" even though Machiavelli notes there is little or nothing in them that can in fact be attributed to fortune (8.35); and Hannibal's inhuman cruelty had the "effect" that he was terrible in the "sight" of his soldiers, even as it is condemned by writers who see it very differently (17.67).

---

[12] See Kenneth Blanchard, "Being, Seeing, Touching: Machiavelli's Modification of Platonic Epistemology," *The Review of Metaphysics* 49, no. 3 (March 1996): 577-607. See also Athanasios Moulakis, "Leo Strauss and Eric Voegelin on Machiavelli," *European Journal of Political Theory* 4, no. 3 (July 2005): 249–262, especially 256.

[13] Blanchard, "Being, Seeing, Touching," 598.

This concern with appearance extends to practical advice, as well. Machiavelli says that each prince should desire *to be held* merciful and not cruel (17.65; emphasis added), and he says that what makes a prince contemptible is *to be held* variable, light, effeminate, pusillanimous, or irresolute (19.72; emphasis added). As a result, a prince should *show himself* as a lover of the traditional virtues, whether or not he actually is such a thing (21.91).

Finally, and most strikingly of all, Machiavelli extends this perspectivalism to the doctrine of the effectual truth itself: "But since my intent is to write something useful to whoever understands it, *it has appeared to me* more fitting to go directly to the effectual truth of the thing than to the imagination of it" (15.61; emphasis added). Why has it appeared to Machiavelli in this way? Perhaps the answer lies in the audience he can expect for a book that is written not in Latin but in the common tongue. "The vulgar," Machiavelli says, "are taken in by the *appearance* and the *outcome* of a thing, and in the world there is no one but the vulgar" (18.70; emphasis added).[14]

In Blanchard's words, echoing Plato's *Protagoras*, "men are governed by fortune over the long run because they are governed by appearances over the short run."[15] The Machiavellian lesson on this point is quite clear: one who wishes not to be governed by fortune must become a master of appear-

---

[14] Though "the vulgar" appears to be a more comprehensive category than the "humor" (*umore*) which Machiavelli calls "the people," it is worth noting that Cesare Borgia is called Duke Valentino both by the people (*chiamato popularmente*; 3.16) and by the vulgar (*chiamato dal vulgo*; 7.26-27). Machiavelli calls him Duke Valentino once (11.46). Montaigne mentions Cesare only a single time in the *Essays* and calls him "the duke of Valentinois" (I.34.163).

[15] Blanchard, 588.

ances, which will help him to become a master of fortune. Beating and striking down fortune requires cruelty, but keeping her down requires deception and a mastery of appearances, i.e., acknowledging that for most people appearances *are* reality. These two conclusions, then, are the heart of the Machiavellian position: for those who wish to conquer fortune, it is necessary to sometimes be cruel and sometimes be deceptive. Hobbes, who follows in Machiavelli's footsteps, puts the point explicitly when he says that the natural state between human beings is war and that "[f]orce and fraud in war are the two cardinal virtues."[16]

Thus it is of little surprise that we are told by Machiavelli, or at least implicitly encouraged, to imitate the actions of Remirro de Orco, a "cruel and ready man" (*uomo crudele ed espedito*; 7.29); the "savage cruelty and inhumanity" of Agathocles (*efferata crudeltà e inumanità*; 8.35), a man who committed "infinite betrayals and cruelties" (*infiniti tradimenti e crudeltà*; 8.37); the "inhuman cruelty" of Hannibal (*inumana crudeltà*; 17.67); the Roman emperors, like Severus Septimus, who were "extremely cruel and rapacious" (*crudelissimi e rapaccissimi*; 19.77-78), the "pious cruelty" of Ferdinand the Catholic (*pietosa crudeltà*; 21.88); and so forth. Machiavelli claims that a prince should not care about the infamy of cruelty (17.65); it is in fact "above all necessary" not to care about having a name for cruelty with one's soldiers (17.67). We are in fact implored to consider, in a jarring juxtaposition, whether there are cruelties well-used (8.37-38) and mercies badly used (17.65)—for example, the "excessive mercy" of Scipio Africanus (17.68). What matters ultimately is not whether one

[16] Thomas Hobbes, *Leviathan*, Part I, Chapter 13, Paragraph 13.

is cruel; rather, it is whether or not any given situation requires one to be considered cruel. At all times, the mastery of appearance is paramount. And thus it is of little surprise that we are told by Machiavelli, or at least implicitly encouraged, to imitate Cesare Borgia, who betrayed Remirro de Orco (7.29-30) and deceived and strangled Vitellozzzo Vitelli (8.37); Cesare's father, Alexander VI, "who never did anything, nor ever thought of anything, but how to deceive men" (18.70); or the ancient writers, who taught "covertly," through the image of Chiron tutoring Achilles, that combat with laws is not always enough and that men must also learn to fight as beasts (18.69).

If fortune must be held down continually, then the horizon of the prince is not Florence or even Italy but rather the theater of operations that Descartes later, in the *Discourse on Method*, calls "this life"—for fortune extends throughout all of this life. And if operating in this life requires a founding act of cruelty and ongoing, thoroughgoing deception, then the "rules for the governments of princes" (DL.4) reduce to rules for being perpetually *en garde*. The thrust of *The Prince* is to look for danger everywhere; to think of the art of war always, even and especially in peace (14.58-60); to reduce the Aristotelian virtue of prudence to paranoia (21.91); to assume that all other men are bad (15.61) or even wicked (17.66-67, 18.69); and so, in order not to come to ruin in this life, to learn how not to be good (15.61, 19.77) or even how to enter into evil (18.70).

All of the heroes of *The Prince*, if we are permitted to so call them, are cruel men or deceivers—and the greatest have allied deception to their cruelty. If all men were good, Machiavelli says, his teaching would not be good. As they are wicked, it is necessary to know well how to be a great pretender and dissembler—for "men are so simple and so obedient to present necessities that he who deceives will always find someone who will let himself be deceived" (18.70). This requirement to be a capable deceiver is why Severus cannot be the highest point of *The Prince,* despite the arguments of some commentators,[17] for Machiavelli tells us that a prince can imitate Severus in order to found his state but that he must imitate Marcus Aurelius at least in part in order to make his principality lasting (19.82). If one wants to hold fortune down, it is indeed first necessary to beat and strike her down, i.e., it is necessary to be cruel. But in order to keep fortune down, it is necessary to be deceptive and to master the subtle techniques that are capable of moving the hearts of all men. Whatever one actually thinks of the project of loving wisdom, one must at least appear to be a philosopher, or perhaps an armed prophet (6.24), in order to avoid a bad end in the long run.

Montaigne and the Love of Truth

Interestingly, it is precisely these two things, cruelty and dishonesty, that Montaigne loathes and that he implores us not to imitate. It is in this way that he takes up Machiavelli's philosophy.

Harvey Mansfield says that *The Prince* is "the most famous book on politics when politics is thought to be carried on for its own sake, unlimited by anything above it."[18] If Montaigne is rejecting Machiavelli and thus rejecting this insubordinate understanding of politics, then we would expect it to be borne out either in deed or in speech, i.e., either in his life or in the

---

[17] For example, Palmer, whose study of *The Prince* in *Masters and Slaves* is otherwise excellent.

[18] See Mansfield's introduction to the second edition of his translation, vii. This essay is reprinted in Mansfield, *Machiavelli's Virtue*, 176-190.

Essays. Montaigne did in fact serve two terms as the mayor of Bordeaux from 1581 to 1585. But in his key political statement—written sometime between 1580 and 1588, and published in 1588—he says in "Of vanity" the following: "I am of the opinion that the most honorable occupation is to serve the public and to be useful [*utile*] to many…For my part, I stay out of it" (III:9,727).[19] He declares that his reluctance to enter political life is partly due to conscience and his imitation of Plato, and partly due to laziness. "I am content," he says, "to enjoy the world without being all wrapped up in it, to live a merely excusable life, which will merely be no burden to myself or others" (III:9,727). Though he bows to obligation upon being elected mayor, Montaigne is content to avoid political life in general; he is content with the "domestic and private" aim he mentions in "To the Reader" (2).[20] After all, as he remarks in "Of repentance," one can "tie up all moral philosophy with a common and private life just as well as with a life of richer stuff. Each man bears the entire form of man's estate" (III:2,611). Neither Montaigne's life nor the project of the *Essays* requires that quality, *polypragmosyne*, which the Greeks ascribed to a busybody. On the contrary, Montaigne says that to him "it is a pleasure not to be concerned in other

[19] Compare III:9,745: "The most useful and honorable science and occupation for a woman is the science of housekeeping."

[20] As Ann Hartle has recently argued, "[t]he action of the *Essays*, then, might be described as bringing the private out into the public…By reordering philosophy to the domestic and private, Montaigne reverses the Aristotelian order." Montaigne's reordering of the Aristotelian priority of the public and the private allows him to present himself in a way that is public but not political. See Ann Hartle, "The Invisibility of Philosophy in the *Essays* of Michel de Montaigne," *The Review of Metaphysics* 65 (June 2012): 800.

people's affairs and to be free of responsibility for them" (III:2,618).

In the aforementioned political statement from "Of vanity," Montaigne admits that politics is both honorable and useful. It should not shock anyone, then, to see politics treated in the first essay of Book III, "Of the useful [*utile*] and the honorable." But what may come as a shock or at least a surprise, especially to those who do not see him as responding to Machiavelli, is that Montaigne makes two clarifying statements: he calls cruelty "so unnatural a vice" (III:1,599); and he says that "[t]he public welfare requires that a man betray and lie and massacre" (III:1,600). Politics, then, is honorable and useful, but the price to be paid for honor and utility is cruelty and treachery. This is neither naïve sanctimony nor moral squeamishness on Montaigne's part; on the contrary, he realizes that deceit has its "proper place" and that it would be "misunderstanding the world" to assert otherwise (III:1,604). But the real philosophical question here is whether one is required to take one's moral bearings from "the world"; whether necessity is a justification for political utility and concomitant moral depravity; whether politics requires one to be above, or even beyond, morality. In a fittingly titled essay, "Of evil means employed to a good end," Montaigne says that we are pushed to such a necessity not by our strength but by the "weakness of our condition" (II:23,518).

Machiavelli says that his intention in *The Prince* is "to write something *useful* [*utile*] to whoever understands it" (15.61; emphasis added). But Montaigne says that "[w]e poorly argue the honor and beauty of an action from its utility [*utilité*], and we commit a fallacy in thinking that everyone is obliged to perform—and that it is honorable to perform—an action merely because it is useful" (*utile*; III:1,610). For Montaigne, cruelty and treachery should not, and indeed cannot, be general rules for human action; taking them as such is to endorse the claim that politics must be the highest human activity. Now, one might wonder whether, its propensity for perniciousness notwithstanding, the Machiavellian position is nonetheless realistic or clear-sighted; if so, morality might be a worthwhile price to pay. But Montaigne asserts that seeing politics in this way leads not to moral clarity but rather to moral bewilderment; it leads to a problematic ranking of the vices and virtues.

In "Of drunkenness," Montaigne says that "[c]onfusion about the order and measurement of sins is dangerous. Murderers, traitors, tyrants gain too much by it" (II:2,244). One of Montaigne's aims in the *Essays* is to rectify this confusion: all vices are equally vices, but they are not all equal vices. As Judith Skhlar notes, Montaigne is the first philosopher to consider cruelty the nadir of the human vices.[21] "Our teachers often rank sins badly," Montaigne says; although he twice says in "Of cruelty [*cruauté*]" that he holds most vices in horror (II:11,311 and 312), he insists that cruelty is the worst: "I cruelly hate cruelty [*Je hay...cruellement la cruauté*], both by nature and by judgment, as the extreme of all vices" (II:11,313). And his hatred of cruelty makes him also hate any imitation of it (III:12,814).

It is striking that Montaigne begins "Of Cruelty" by distinguishing between virtue and goodness, a distinction for which

[21] See Judith N. Shklar, *Ordinary Vices* (Cambridge: Harvard University Press, 1985) especially chapter 1. The title of her book is an homage to Montaigne's comment in "Of Cannibals" that "treachery, disloyalty, tyranny, and cruelty" are "our ordinary vices" (I.31.156).

Machiavelli is notorious. In a related essay—"Cowardice, mother of cruelty [*cruauté*]"—Montaigne says that he has often heard that cowardice is the mother of cruelty and that he has found "by experience that the bitterness and hardness of a malicious and inhuman heart are usually accompanied by feminine weakness" (II:27,523). In a third essay, "Of the punishment of cowardice," he distinguishes between vices that come from malice and those that come from weakness, although he admits that extraordinary cowardice should be taken as wicked and malicious and as a result punished accordingly (I:16,48). The implication of these three essays, when taken together, seems to be that the separation of virtue from goodness leads to cowardice—and that cowardice leads to wickedness, malice, and cruelty. Goodness without virtue can be weak; it can be saccharine and sentimental. But virtue without goodness can be cruel—as when Montaigne says that it is cruel for ancient philosophy to demand "so composed a bearing" in "extreme accidents," such as having kidney stones (II:37,577). Excessive philosophic virtue is a cruelty to ourselves (1:39,179).

But what is more problematic to Montaigne than cruelty to ourselves is cruelty toward others, which is why he has been lauded by contemporary liberal thinkers such as Skhlar and Richard Rorty. On this point, Montaigne's moral circle extends quite a distance; it includes not only our daily and social interactions with others but political issues such as justice, as well. He says in at least two places that all that goes beyond plain death is cruelty (II:11,314 and II:27,530), and he even goes so far as to lament what he calls the "inhuman excesses" of torture (II:11,315). He decries the pagan practice of human sacrifice (I:130,149 and II:12,387), a practice that assumes the cruelty of the gods.[22] But he also says that nothing in the ancient histories is more extreme than what is experienced in his time every day "through the license of our civil wars" (II:11,315). To murder for the mere pleasure of it; to hack off limbs; to create ingenious tortures; to enjoy the groans of the dying—this is the "uttermost point that cruelty can attain" (II:11,316).

These passages, together with those above, show that cruelty is the worst of vices for Montaigne. However, it is not his sole moral concern. He hates not only cruelty but also deception, and he finds honesty and truth to be of paramount importance both for an individual life and for society in general. Remarking upon the "new-fangled virtue of hypocrisy and dissimulation [*nouvelle vertu de faintise et de dissimulation*]," Montaigne is blunt and to the point: "I mortally hate it" (*je la hay capitallement*; II:17,491) It is a moral quality that is "so highly honored at present" but which, "of all vices," testifies to "so much cowardice and baseness of heart" (II:17,491). Here we see Montaigne's humor or at least his sarcasm: dissimulation is one of these new "virtues" without goodness, which is to say it is not a virtue at all but rather a vice. Furthermore, we see that cowardice is not only the mother of cruelty but that it is also a cause of deception. As Montaigne continues, "[i]t is a craven and servile idea to disguise ourselves and hide under a mask, and not to dare to show ourselves as we are" (II:17,491). He calls lying an "accursed vice" (I:9,23) and an "ugly vice" (II:18,505), and he says that fraud and trickery make for a malicious justice (III:1,600).

---

[22] Ann Hartle, "Montaigne's Accidental Moral Philosophy," *Philosophy and Literature* 24 (No.1, April 2000): 150.

Nietzsche calls Montaigne "the freest and mightiest of souls" and says: "I know of only one writer whom I would compare with Schopenhauer, indeed set above him, in respect of honesty: Montaigne."[23] Montaigne consistently and repeatedly upholds honesty throughout the *Essays*. He says in "To the Reader" that he wants to be seen in his "simple, natural, ordinary fashion" (2), and he claims that we "hold together only by our word" (I:9,23). He says that "[t]ruth is the first and fundamental part of virtue" (II:17,491) and that "the first stage in the corruption of morals is the banishment of truth" (II:18,505). His own age is suffused with a love of deception, but Montaigne says that "[p]ure naturalness and truth, in whatever age, still find their time and their place" (III:1,600). Whatever the variable guise of legal constraint, the "law of honesty" binds Montaigne tightly (III:9,738).

Montaigne implies that his bad memory makes him unfit for deception (I:29,32; see also II:17.,92). He says that his honest face twice saved him from danger (III:12,813 and III:12,814). "I have an open way," he says, "that easily insinuates itself and gains credit on first acquaintance" (III:1,600)—and "an open way of speaking opens up another man's speech and draws it out, as do wine and love" (III:1,602). On occasion, one does detect a sensitivity to audience, a sense of public artifice: "I speak the truth, not my fill of it, but as much as I dare speak" (III:2,611).[24] Further,

---

[23] From "Schopenhauer as educator" in Friedrich Nietzsche, *Untimely Meditations*, trans. R.J. Hollingdale (Cambridge: Cambridge University Press, 1990) 135.

[24] Montaigne offers the following "amusing notion" regarding the question of audience: "...many things that I would not want to tell anyone, I tell the public; and for my most secret knowledge and thoughts I send my

remarking upon quotation, Montaigne says: "I, among so many borrowings of mine, am very glad to be able to hide one now and then, disguising and altering it for a new service" (III:12,809). But typically he insists that he does not engage in irony or subtlety in speech or in deed, and that those who think he does are mistaken: "Surely they make my subtlety too subtle" (III:1,603), he says with more than a hint of dryness.[25]

Though he admits that "this whole procedure" of his is "just a bit dissonant from our ways" (III:1,603), Montaigne refuses to depart from it. He is "singularly scrupulous about lying" and will give whoever asks the "naked and unvarnished truth" (III:11,786); he is "scrupulous to the point of superstition" in keeping his promises (III:9,738); he feels shame and remorse if a lie escapes his lips, as his "soul by nature shuns lying and hates even to think a lie" (II:17,491); he would rather be "troubling and indiscreet than flattering and dissembling" (II:17,492); he is an "enemy of subtle and dissimulated acts and hate[s] trickery" in himself (I:21,71); he laments the "malicious dishonesty and deceit" that spring up in childhood, that form the foundation of "our greatest vices," and that are the "true seeds and roots of cruelty, tyranny, and treason" (I:23,78); and he always had an "aversion for mixing trickery or ruse" in his childish games, preferring to stick to his "straight

---

most faithful friends to a bookseller's shop" (III:9,750). See also III:11,785: "I am ordinarily obliged to play the fool for company's sake and discuss frivolous subjects and stories which I entirely disbelieve."

25 For a different interpretation of Montaigne's philosophy—one that focuses on the theme of Montaigne's subtlety—see David Lewis Schaefer, *The Political Philosophy of Montaigne* (Ithaca: Cornell University Press, 1990). See also David R. Hiley, "The Politics of Skepticism: Reading Montaigne," *History of Philosophy Quarterly* (Vol.9, No.4, October 1992): 379-399.

and open road" which he follows "by a natural and unstudied propensity, an extreme repugnance to cheating" (I.23.79). It is "painful for him to dissemble" (III.5.642), and he hates either to deceive or to see anyone deceived in him (III.1.600). "By nature," he says, "I find it hard to communicate myself by halves and moderately, and with that servile and suspicious` prudence that is prescribed to us..." (III.3.623). Machiavelli says that it is "always more useful [*utile*]" to be a "true friend and a true enemy" than to remain neutral between warring parties (21.89). But Montaigne says that "nothing keeps us from getting along comfortably and in good faith between two hostile parties" (III.1.602). Though "double-dealing men are useful [*utiles*]," Montaigne says that "[t]here is no reason of utility [*utilité*] for which I would permit myself to lie" to any given pair of rivals (III.1.602).

Though Montaigne hates both cruelty and deception, he finds the latter the most socially destructive. Truth is the foundation and virtue of society, and deception ruins the social fabric by making human beings unable to trust one another. "Since mutual understanding is brought about solely by words," Montaigne says, "he who breaks his word betrays human society" (II.18.505). Machiavelli's new virtue of dissimulation is ultimately the most cowardly of vices, and thus is the most malicious, because it makes utility the standard of moral action and because it undermines the grounds for the possibility of a functioning society. There is no virtue helped by falsehood (II.6.274), and Montaigne says that "[n]o worse state of things can be imagined than where wickedness comes to be legitimate and, with the leave of the authorities, assumes the cloak of virtue" (III.12.798). Montaigne notes that no less of an authority than Plato said that the "extreme of injustice" occurs when "what is unjust is held to be just" (III:12,798).

Nature and Fortune

Cruelty and deception are the requirements for Machiavelli's prince to conquer fortune, and cruelty and deception are precisely the two things that Montaigne excoriates repeatedly and in the strongest possible terms. Since Montaigne rejects the Machiavellian results, we might expect him to reject the Machiavellian premise, i.e., that we should conquer fortune.

Is this in fact true of Montaigne? One way to begin to address this question is ask whether Montaigne, following Machiavelli, sees all things as being variable and in motion.[26] Though it is doubtful whether Montaigne would go so far as to say that the world is simply matter in motion (Galileo) or that life is simply a motion of limbs (Hobbes), he does say in "Of drunkenness" that "[t]he world is nothing but variety and dissimilarity" (II:22,244). As Donald Frame notes, "[f]or

[26] Of course, to say that the cosmos is in constant motion or constantly changing is not necessarily a modern position. Lucretius, for instance, is cited many times in the *Essays*, and Montaigne lists him as one of his four top poets in "Of books" (II:10,298). See M.A. Screech, *Montaigne's annotated copy of Lucretius: a transcription of the manuscript, notes, and pen-marks* (Genève: Droz, 1998). As Frame notes in his Introduction to his translation of the *Essays*, Montaigne is sometimes taken to have had an "epicurean period" lasting from 1578 to 1592 (xii). The most recent work on Machiavelli's indebtedness to Epicurus is Robert J. Roecklein *Machiavelli and Epicureanism: An Investigation into the Origins of Modern Political Thought* (Lexington: Lexington Books, 2012). See also W.R. Newell, "How Original is Machiavelli?: A Consideration of Skinner's Interpretation of Virtue and Fortune," *Political Theory* (Vol. 15, No. 4, Nov. 1987): 612-634.

Montaigne, everything here below is becoming and not being, appearance and not reality."[27] Though Montaigne does not believe that the world is random or accidental (II:23,516), he does speak of it as if it were nothing but ceaseless flux: "The world is but a perennial movement. All things in it are in constant motion—the earth, the rocks of the Caucasus, the pyramids of Egypt—both with the common motion and with their own. Stability itself is nothing but a more languid motion" (III:2,610). Montaigne does not seem to believe that there is a natural pattern of things, that there is something unchangeable beneath the motion of natural phenomena.

Human phenomena seem similarly unstable for Montaigne. He can conceive of "a thousand contrary ways of life" (I:37,169) and thus has "a singular desire that we should each be judged in ourselves apart, and that [he] may not be measured in conformity with the common patterns (I:37,169).[28] There is an "infinite diversity of human action" which is in "perpetual motion" (III:13,815), and "there is nothing stable in us" (II:23,517). Montaigne consistently speaks of the instability and changeability of all human beings, including himself.[29] And he consistently speaks as if he were only interested in characterizing change, only interested in telling of the surface or ephemerality of things, as when he says: "I do not portray being; I portray passing" (III:2,611).

---

[27] Donald M. Frame, *Montaigne's Discovery of Man: The Humanization of a Humanist* (New York: Columbia University Press, 1955) 9.

[28] It is worth noting that, by the very end of the *Essays*, these common human patterns have become "the common human pattern" (III.13.857).

[29] Ann Hartle, "Sticking to the Old Ways: Montaigne and Sacred Tradition," *Anamnesis* 1 (No.1, 2011): 45.

For Montaigne, all things are in flux; nothing is fixed in nature, even when we extend the idea of "nature" to include human beings. Since nothing is fixed, nature appears variable; it appears as the wiles of fortune. And since it appears to us as fortune, one might say that it is in effect reducible to fortune.[30] Montaigne thus agrees with Machiavelli's general assessment that nature looks like fortune. However, Montaigne's response to that assessment differs markedly from that of Machiavelli. Though Montaigne speaks of "[t]he inconstant and variable movement of Fortune" which makes her "necessarily present all sorts of faces" (I:34,163) and though he admits that the best of his bodily qualities is that he is "flexible and not very stubborn" (III:13,830), his notion of flexibility with respect to the variability of fortune is quite different than that of Machiavelli.

The *Essays* include frequent references to fortune. Indeed, Montaigne regularly speaks of the *Essays* themselves as arising from fortune or chance. When choosing a topic, he says that he "take[s] the first subject that chance offers" (I:50,219). Regarding his many citations, he remarks, "I have no other marshal but fortune to arrange my bits" (II:10,297). Sometimes, he digresses, as when he discusses Seneca's view of philosophy near the end of "Not to counterfeit being sick"—but this is acceptable for him, since "there is profit in change" (II:25,522). He contrasts the artfulness of musical composition to his own, saying that the former is "guided by art, mine by chance" (III:2,611).

Montaigne progressively takes on a more favorable view toward fortune throughout the course of the *Essays*. He is always accepting of fortune, but by the end of the work he

[30] Mansfield, *Machiavelli's Virtue*, 129.

seems to think it does him favors even when it provides him with woes. In Book I, he distances himself from the project of conquering fortune or even preparing for future contingencies. "It is enough for me," he says, "while under fortune's favor, to prepare for its disfavor" (I:39,179). However, he remains ambivalent as to fortune's benefits: "Our good and our ill depend on ourselves alone. Let us offer our offerings and vows to ourselves, not to Fortune; she has no power over our character; on the contrary, it drags her in its train and molds her in its own form" (I:50,220). Later, he has become more appreciative as well as more nonchalant and lax: "Fortune pays me properly" (III:2,618), and "…I have declared war to the death against all care" (III:9,741). And by the end of Book III and thus the end of the *Essays*, he goes so far as to say that he is fortune's "servant" (III:12,801) and the "sort of man who readily commits himself to Fortune and abandons himself bodily into her arms" (III:12,812). He says that he has found fortune "both wiser and more friendly" to his affairs than he has been (III:12,812), and he even says that he is "obliged to Fortune for assailing [him] so often with the same kind of weapons" (III.13.837).

This attitude is the result of a long tarrying with fortune. Montaigne notes that philosophers who have desired to marry intellectual virtue with the willingness to act "have not been content to await the rigors of Fortune in shelter and repose, for fear she might surprise them inexperienced and new to the combat; rather they have gone forth to meet her and have flung themselves deliberately into the test of difficulties" (II:6,267). For "[w]e become hardened to whatever we are accustomed to" (III:9,741), and those that do not habituate themselves to difficulty, who do not prepare themselves for fortune's wiles, are at the mercy of her. Montaigne says that we should be grateful when fortune puts us to the test (III:1,800). But it is more praiseworthy to seek out fortune and put her to the test, as did Epaminondas, Socrates, and the Stoics and Epicureans (II:11,307). Montaigne thus suggests that we can prepare ourselves for fortune, which is a very different sense of flexibility than we see in Machiavelli. Machiavelli's teaching is that we should reduce the variability of fortune by conquering her; Montaigne's teaching is that we accustom ourselves to her variability. He would agree with Machiavelli, however, that we risk constant turmoil and even disaster if we simply do nothing. Responding to "very magnificent and beautiful words" of Lucretius, Montaigne notes that "a very slight accident put this man's understanding into a worse state than that of the lowest shepherd, notwithstanding that Teacher-God [Epicurus] of his and that divine wisdom" (II:12,360). Speaking of his best friend, Montaigne says:

> And the greatest man I have known in person, I mean for natural qualities of the soul, and the best endowed, was Etienne La Boétie. He was truly a full soul, handsome from every point of view; a soul of the old stamp, who would have achieved great results if fortune had willed it, for he had added much to this rich nature by learning and study (II:17,500).

La Boétie had the potential to do great things, but the lesson is that even such a man could not completely avoid the role of fortune in his life. Habituation to her wiles is therefore crucial.

On this point, it is worth pondering whether fortune can actually be conquered or whether this is the noble lie of *The Prince*. Machiavelli speaks of both himself (DL.4) and of Cesare Borgia (7.27) as suffering from awful misfortunes—the latter in one of the memorable passages in the book.

Machiavelli says in his own name that he does not know what better teaching he could give to a new prince than the example of Cesare Borgia's actions, which included laying for himself great foundations (7.27) and deciding to depend no longer on the arms and fortune of others (7.28). Despite this praiseworthy preparation, Cesare is ruined by an "extraordinary and extreme malignity of fortune" (7.27). This misfortune was not the death of his powerful father, Pope Alexander VI; Cesare had thought of that in advance and had found a remedy for almost every contingency associated with it. But not everything can be calculated. In one of only two places in *The Prince* where Machiavelli appears as a character,[31] Cesare tells Machiavelli that he had never thought that when his father was dying that he would be dying, too (7.32).

In an essay entitled "Fortune is often met in the path of reason," Montaigne relates this story in somewhat more humorous fashion and surely intends to respond to Machiavelli's version of it in *The Prince*. It is the only essay which contains the word "fortune" in the title, and it is also the only one in which Montaigne mentions Cesare Borgia and Alexander VI, either singly or together. He tells their tale as the first of nine

---

[31] The other instance occurs at 3.16. During the occasion of Cesare Borgia's occupation of Romagna and during Machiavelli's first diplomatic mission to France, Machiavelli speaks with the cardinal of Rouen. The cardinal says that the Italians do not understand war; Machiavelli replies that the French do not understand the state. Compare 14.58: "Thus, a prince should have no other object, nor any other thought, nor take anything else as his art but that of war and its orders and discipline; for that is the only art which is of concern to one who commands." Compare also the 10 December 1513 letter to Vettori: "[T]hrough this thing [*The Prince*], if it were read, one would see that I have neither slept through nor played away the fifteen years I have been at the study of the art of the state."

anecdotes, and like Machiavelli, he relates the fact of Alexander VI's death. But he offers a version that differs importantly from that of Machiavelli; in Montaigne's version, Cesare is responsible for killing his own father. The details are simultaneously grim and amusing. Cesare had resolved to poison Adrian, the cardinal of Corneto, with whom he and Alexander were going to dine, and thus sent a poisoned bottle of wine ahead of him to the meal. The butler was told to watch over the bottle carefully; however, he believed this was only due to the wine's excellence, and as a result later served it to Alexander. Cesare, trusting that his poisoned bottle would have not have been served, mistakenly drank some, as well. The result was that Alexander died immediately and that Cesare grew very ill and hovered near death himself. Thus, in the only mention of Cesare and Alexander in all of the *Essays*, Montaigne tells us that what Machiavelli calls the "extreme and extraordinary malignity of fortune" (7.27) suffered by Cesare was to have accidentally poisoned both himself and his father. "Is there a more express act of justice than this one" (I.34.162), Montaigne wonders—and one can imagine the smile on his face.

Machiavelli says that fortune, when she wants to make new princes great, will supply opportunities for them to demonstrate their greatness (20.85).[32] However, it appears that the opposite is also the case; as Montaigne says, "[s]ometimes it seems that Fortune deliberately plays with us" (I:34,163). Just as storms and tempests level our proud buildings, "it seems that Fortune sometimes lies in wait precisely for the last day of our

[32] As Palmer notes, this is the first time that Machiavelli humanizes fortune by saying "she" (88).

life, to show her power to overturn in a moment what she has built up over many years…" (I:19,54-5). Montaigne points out the mundane or even bizarre deaths of many men of note: Aeschylus dying from a tortoise shell being dropped on his head by an eagle; Aemilius Lepidus dying by stumbling against his threshold; Speusippus and even "one of our Popes"[33] dying between "women's thighs"; Montaigne's own brother dying from being hit in the head with a tennis ball. Montaigne tells of men being killed by grape seeds, hair combs, the charge of a hog, the stifling of a crowd, and even the door of a council chamber. "With such frequent and ordinary examples passing before our eyes," he exclaims, "how can we possibly rid ourselves of the thought of death and of the idea that at every moment it is gripping us by the throat" (I:20,59)? Life is such a "tender thing and easy to disturb" (III:9,725), and death has so many ways to "surprise us" (I:20,58).

Modernity and Death

The concern with fortune in Machiavelli and Montaigne, thus, is really a concern with death. One way to understand modern philosophy, or at least modern political philosophy, is in this difference of opinion between Machiavelli and Montaigne regarding the appropriate attitude toward fortune and, consequently, death. As Leo Strauss has noted, ancient political philosophy recognizes that the realization or instantiation of the best regime is ineluctably dependent upon chance. Modern political philosophy denies this dependence—and the claim

---

[33] Montaigne's phrase, "one of our Popes," perhaps refers to Pope John XII (955–963) who was killed by an enraged husband while in the act of committing adultery with the man's wife.

that Machiavelli upholds, if not inaugurates, modern political philosophy is one that has been suggested frequently by Strauss.[34]

Much of the force and plausibility of this claim depends upon what the word "modern" means, though it is beyond our scope to investigate the many and varied answers to this question. I am inclined to agree with Stanley Rosen's assessment that "[m]odernity is not simply a historical period but a metaphysical condition of the human spirit."[35] What is this condition? Rosen notes that it is possible to characterize it as upholding the project "to free mankind from the bonds of religion and to employ the methods of mathematical reasoning to resolve ethical and political problems."[36] The former aim is particularly important for our purposes. Whatever modernity is, the desire to emancipate human beings from religion is central to almost every manifestation of it, with modern political philosophy being perhaps the most outstanding specimen.

---

[34] See Leo Strauss, *What is Political Philosophy? And Other Studies* (Chicago: University of Chicago Press, 1989) 40-49; *The Political Philosophy of Hobbes: Its Basis and Genesis* (Chicago: University of Chicago Press, 1963) xv; *An Introduction to Political Philosophy: Ten Essays of Leo Strauss*, edited by Hilail Gildin (Detroit: Wayne State Press, 1989) 83-89; *On Tyranny*, revised and expanded edition, edited by Victor Gourevitch and Michael S. Roth (Chicago: University of Chicago Press, 2000) 25; and *History of Political Philosophy*, third edition, edited by Leo Strauss and Joseph Cropsey (Chicago: University of Chicago Press, 1987) 297. See also Clifford Orwin, "Machiavelli's Unchristian Charity," *American Political Science Review* 72 (1978): 1217-1228. Contrast Anthony J. Parel, *The Machiavellian Cosmos* (New Haven: Yale University Press, 1992) 158.

[35] Stanley Rosen, "Leo Strauss and the Problem of the Modern," in *The Cambridge Companion to Leo Strauss* (Cambridge: Cambridge University Press, 2009) 121.

[36] Ibid., 120.

Another way to put this point is to say that modern philosophy is obsessed with death. The fear of, or at least the preoccupation with, death has always concerned, if not haunted, all but the most superficial of philosophical authors. But this fear becomes particularly pointed in thinkers given to reject ideas of transcendence, of the afterlife, and of the immortality of the soul—thinkers whose concern with non-existence becomes as a result exacerbated rather than disarmed. In its retreat from transcendence, modern philosophy inadvertently makes death its primary concern. Just as Heidegger quips that an atheist is someone who thinks about God all the time, one might suggest that a modern philosopher is someone who thinks about death all the time. What is most clear and distinct to the modern mind is not mathematics but rather the discomfort and disquietude attendant to the contemplation of one's demise.

In the 10 December 1513 letter to Vettori, Machiavelli offers a poignant portrait of his evening routine, which occurs after he has spent his day among the "vermin" of his estate:

> When evening has come, I return to my house and go into my study. At the door I take off my clothes of the day, covered with mud and mire, and I put on my regal and courtly garments; and decently reclothed, I enter the ancient courts of ancient men, where, received by them lovingly, I feed on the food that alone is mine and that I was born for. There I am not ashamed to speak with them and to ask them the reason for their actions; and they in their humanity reply to me. And for the space of four hours I feel no boredom, I forget every pain, I do not fear poverty, *death does not frighten me*. I deliver myself entirely to them (109-110; emphasis added).[37]

---

[37] Compare 14.57: "I submit myself entirely to these orders."

Aristotle notes that there were three ways known to antiquity of escaping the human condition of mortality: the abandonment in pure pleasure; the celestial rapture of philosophical contemplation; and the etching of oneself into the memories of men by the performance of great deeds.[38] For four hours an evening, Machiavelli engages in a form of each of these three ancient modes. Only then does he achieve a kind of quietude, a tranquility that is denied him in his everyday life. The Christian religion seemed to hold no relief for him; Quentin Skinner asserts that there is no evidence to support the tale that Machiavelli summoned a priest to his deathbed to hear a final confession.[39] It is only the contemplation of the great deeds of the ancient world that provides Machiavelli existential solace. The paradox of modern political philosophy, if we take Machiavelli to be archetypal of it, is that it denies the premises of ancient philosophy while remaining desirous of its benefits.

Montaigne's attitude is very different; the thing he fears most is fear, not death (I:18,53). Whether this is because he prefers ancient books to modern ones (II:10,297)[40] or because

[38] Aristotle, *Nicomachean Ethics*, second edition, trans. Terence Irwin, Hackett, 1999. 1095b12-1096a5.

[39] Quentin Skinner, *Machiavelli: A Brief Insight* (New York: Sterling, 2010) 140. Regarding the status of Machiavelli's "Exhortation to Penitence," see Theodore A. Sumberg, "Machiavelli's Sermon on Penance," *Perspectives on Political Science* 23 (Fall 1994): 171-173; Dante Germino, "Second Thoughts on Leo Strauss' Machiavelli," *Journal of Politics* 28 (1966): 794-817; and Mansfield, *Machiavelli's Virtue*, 222-223.

[40] It is worth noting that Montaigne does not like Greek works (II.10.297) although the implication is that he does not properly understand them. But there is also a question of taste; he is not enamored of Aristotle's style and laments that even Plato's dialogues drag on too much (II:10,301). Even some Roman authors are not spared; Montaigne says that

he is sincere and constant in his Catholic faith (II.12.428),[41] he is more than comfortable with the idea of mortality. Montaigne says that death is "a part of our being no less essential than life" (III:12,807). He tells the reader that it is the "condition of your creation; it is a part of you; you are fleeing from your own selves. This being of yours that you enjoy is equally divided between death and life. The first day of your birth leads you toward death as toward life" (I:20,65). Heidegger might say that human being is being toward death. Montaigne goes farther: human being is also being toward life. It is the human condition to oscillate between these poles, to exist in a tension between natality and mortality; he says that "Nature teaches us that she has made us for living and dying alike…" (II:6,268). Whatever the anxieties or dreams of modern philosophy, there is no escape from this condition for Montaigne; death is universal and inevitable (III:12,802 and I:20,57), and "Nature forces us to it" (I:20,65). It is more than a mere condition, however; it is a purpose. Death is indeed the terminus of life (III:12,805). But it is also "[t]he goal" (I:20,57), the "necessary object" (I:20,57), and "[t]he constant work" of life (I:20,65). It is "the remedy for all ills" (II:3,252) and, perhaps most importantly for our purposes, "the origin of another life" (I:20,64).

Young and old, healthy and sick, all die; Montaigne notes that neither Christ nor "the greatest man that was simply a

---

Cicero's "way of writing, and every other similar way, seems to [him] boring" (II.10.301).

[41] See Hartle, "Montaigne and Sacred Tradition," 45. See also Frame, *Montaigne's Discovery of Man*, 9: "One realm that Montaigne always places beyond doubt is the Catholic religion. Even the critics who think he undermines it see no change in his attitude."

man"—Alexander the Great—lived beyond the age of 33. Things that may at first glance appear to hasten our demise, such as illnesses, are therefore not problematic for Montaigne; they may in fact have some benefit. He praises plague victims for their resoluteness and equanimity in the face of mortality (III:12,802). When speaking of allowing illnesses to run their course in his body, Montaigne notes that "you do not die of being sick, you die of being alive. Death kills you well enough without the help of illness" (III:13,837). By getting rid of some illnesses, we eliminate opportunities to reflect upon death—Montaigne's kidney stones being the most obvious example. Having that particular affliction means that "[i]f you do not embrace death, at least you shake hands with it once a month" (III:13,837). Such conditions—milder than the plague, but still potentially fatal—grant us a familiarity, a closeness to death. "It is not so much that I keep aloof from the thought of being dead," Montaigne says, "as that I enter into familiar terms with dying" (III:9,742).

Montaigne ridicules the pretensions of philosophers with respect to death. "Philosophy," he says, "orders us to have death ever before our eyes, to foresee and consider it before the time comes, and afterward gives us rules and precautions to provide against our being wounded by this foresight and thought" (III.12.804). For most people, the torment of this preparation is worse than death itself. There is no need for morbid brooding; dying is "the greatest task we have to perform," but "practice cannot help us" (II:6,267). Besides, as Montaigne says in one of his more humorous remarks, learning to die in the Platonic sense is superfluous: "If you don't know how to die, don't worry; Nature will tell you what to do on the spot, fully and adequately. She will do this job perfectly for you; don't bother your head about it" (III:12,804). By contrast, Montaigne praises the way that ignorant people meet death at least as admirably as any philosopher. "Should I have died less cheerfully before having read the *Tusculans*? I think not,"[42] Montaigne asserts (III:12,794). Nature's arguments will suffice to make a "peasant" and even "whole nations" die as "steadfastly as a philosopher" (III:12,794).

This point requires further explication. One cannot practice dying, but one can prepare for death by becoming habituated to its presence. In this sense, Montaigne's sense of philosophy is perhaps closest to that of Plato, for, like Plato, he possesses a nuanced understanding of ignorance. It is true, as mentioned above, that Montaigne praises ignorance over philosophical learning when it comes to understanding mortality. For ignorance to work, however, one must listen to the voice of Nature (III:12,794). To refuse to do so is to suffer something akin to what on the Platonic account would be the most contemptible stupidity.[43] Montaigne says that "[w]e are all of the common herd" (II:12,429) and that the "remedy of the common herd" is to refuse to think about death (II:20,57-58). "But what brutish stupidity can come from so gross a blindness," Montaigne exclaims (I:20,58). "These people" become frightened at the "mere mention of death" (I:20,58). Montaigne's solution is to tarry with death always but never to be frightened or worried about it (I:20,59). The trick is how to chart a middle course between morbid obsession and complete avoidance, how to cultivate a sort of learned ignorance or nonchalance. The trick is somehow to rethink what is

[42] Cicero's *Tusculan Disputations.*
[43] See for instance *Alcibiades* 118a.

common, to begin in wonder at the common but still end in ignorance (III:11,788).

Montaigne critiques the "brutish nonchalance" (I:20,59) that faces death in cowardly fashion. Cowardice, though it generates cruelty and treachery, might be acceptable if it led to immortality. However, it does not; death "catches you just the same, whether you flee like a coward or act like a man" (I:20,59). We must rid ourselves of cowardly thoughts of death—of these "vulgar and harmful humors" (I:20,62)—and we must become habituated to the idea of death as early as possible. "Let us learn to meet it steadfastly and to combat it," Montaigne says, and let us "await it everywhere" (I:20,60). The premeditation of death is the premeditation of freedom, and "he who has learned how to die has unlearned how to be a slave. Knowing how to die frees us from all subjection and constraint" (I:20,60). It is the only way to have peace, for it is "impossible for the soul to be at rest while she fears death" (I:20,63). For Montaigne, learning to die is not to disavow the body in order to focus on the soul. It is instead to become habituated to the idea that the body will perish without despising the body for that fact (III:13,849; see also III:13,855).

Montaigne constantly attends to death and makes it a part of his life: "I have formed the habit of having death continually present" (I:20,62). He says that he dreams of death all the time (I:20,60), and says that every minute he seems to be "constantly slipping away" from himself (I:20,61). There is "nothing he investigates so eagerly" or so "attentively" in histories as the death of men (I:20,62). In "Of practice," he relates his own near-death experience upon being knocked from his horse by another rider, suffering the only swoon he had experienced at the time of writing (II:6,269). He says that a swoon or faint leads one "very close to seeing death's true and natural face" (II:6,268), the "face and idea of death so true to nature" (II:6,269). This experience has allowed him to familiarize himself with death and even try it out to some extent (II:6,268), and he says that "there is nothing like coming close to it" (II:6,272).

This constant attention to death gives Montaigne a marked, but not a "brutish," nonchalance toward living and dying. "[N]ever did a man so distrust his life" (I:20,61), Montaigne says, and never was a man readier for death: "Since I am constantly brooding over my thoughts and settling them within me, I am at all times about as well prepared as I can be. And the coming of death will teach me nothing new" (I.20.61). He wanted death to find him planting his cabbages, "careless of death" and still more careless of his unfinished garden (I:20,62).

The *Essays* themselves can be taken as an enormous testament to this attitude. In a statement that appears to strike to the heart of the intentionality behind the *Essays*, he says: "If I were a maker of books, I would make a register, with comments, of various deaths. He who would teach men to die would teach them to live" (I:20,62). The essay in which this statement is made is of course called "That to philosophize is to learn to die," and the *Essays* themselves as a result appear as just this register, just this record of how men learn to live by learning to die—with Montaigne's life and death standing as the premier examples. "It is not my deeds that I write down; it is myself, it is my essence" (II:6,274). Montaigne's *Essays* are a record both of learning to die and learning to live. He did not want his death to say anything that his life had not said; unlike

Machiavelli, Montaigne died in his home at Mass at the elevation of the Host.[44]

Vanity and Wisdom

What remains is to say a few words about the type of life that Montaigne's stance toward death recommends. Montaigne says that "it is living happily, not, as Antisthenes said, dying happily, that constitutes human felicity" (III:2,619). So how does Montaigne's attitude toward death shape his attitude toward life? Montaigne does not say that we should become "like God" or that we should flee from "here to there," as Socrates does in Plato's *Theaetetus*. On the contrary, Montaigne says that "supercelestial thoughts" are often in "singular accord" with "subterranean conduct" (III:13,856). The "madness" of philosophers trying to get outside of themselves, to raise themselves, becomes instead a lowering: "instead of changing into angels, they change into beasts" (III:13,856). We should not try to become God, to become literally divine. Rather, "[i]t is an absolute perfection and virtually divine [*comme divine*] to know how to enjoy our being rightfully" (III:13,857).[45]

But our being—human being—is a strange thing. As Montaigne says: "I have seen no more evident monstrosity and miracle in the world than myself" (III:17,787). Our "peculiar condition" is that we are as fit to be laughed at as able to laugh (I:50,221); echoing Ecclesiastes, Montaigne speaks of the "nullity of man's estate" (II:6,275) and asserts that we are all

---

[44] Hartle, "Sticking to the Olds Ways: Montaigne and Sacred Tradition," 61. See also Frame's introduction to his translation, xii.

[45] Screech translates *comme divine* as "as it were God-like." See Screech, *The Complete Essays*, 1268.

wind (III:13,849), smoke (II:12,360), and "not so full of evil as of inanity" (I:51,221). And yet this emptiness is not to be despised: "We are great fools. 'He has spent his life in idleness,' we say; 'I have done nothing today.' What, have you not lived?" (III:13,850). The vanity of life does not lead to despair for Montaigne; he says that "the most barbarous of our maladies is to despise our being" (III:13,852). Rather, the contingency of life leads to a joyfulness, a delight in the existence of things that do not have to exist. The overall tone of the *Essays* is that of being pleasantly surprised by almost everything and of being amused that there is anything at all.

Montaigne says that he "love[s] life and cultivate[s] it just as God has been pleased to grant it to us" (III:13,854) and that his "intention is to pass pleasantly, and not laboriously, what life" he has left (II:10,297). He has few or no regrets about his life and states that he would live the same life were he to have a chance to live again (III:2,620). He contrasts Democritus, who found the condition of man "vain and ridiculous," with Heraclitus, who was "perpetually sad" (I:50,220), and says that he prefers the Democritean path of laughter. It is not only that laughter is pleasanter but that it is "more disdainful," more inclined to see life as foolish (I:50,221). Montaigne says that "[w]e should spread joy, but cut down sadness as much as we can (III:9,748) and begins the essay, "Of sadness, by proclaiming that he is "one of those freest from this passion" (I:2,6).[46] On the contrary, he says he "do[es] nothing without gaiety…" (II:10,297). Montaigne says that we hate what we take seriously (I:50,221), so he tries to avoid taking anything seriously—such as chess, which he "hate[s]" and "avoid[s]"

[46] Compare I:38,173-174.

because it is "not enough of a game, and too serious an amusement" (I:50,220). Taking something seriously means that one's happiness is a function of that thing. Montaigne says that the poor, exiles, and slaves "often live as joyfully as other men" (I:18,53), and the suggestion is that this is because they are liberated from the love of one's own—from the love of one's possessions, one's country, one's freedom, or even one's life.

In one of the most important passages in the *Essays*, Montaigne says that the "surest sign of wisdom [*sagesse*] is a constant cheerfulness [*une esjouïssance constante*];" it is an "ever serene state" like that of the "things above the moon" (I:26,119). The *Essays* end with an invocation to Apollo, and the last prose words of the *Essays* are "gay and sociable wisdom" (*sagesse, mais gaye et sociale*; III:13,857). It is because Montaigne is ever ready to die that he sees life for what it is—empty and pretentious, yet humorous and delightful. On the loftiest throne in the world, we are still sitting only on our own rump (III:13,857), but it is not to be despised for all that.

It is this joyfulness that in the end most fully distinguishes Montaigne from Machiavelli. Machiavelli lays the foundations for the understanding of modern life as the joyless quest for joy.[47] He is no mere grand acquisitor; there is indeed humor in Machiavelli, and it is too often forgotten that he wrote comedies. But he rarely, if ever, laughs at himself and at his mortality, and it is only in contemplation of the great deeds of ancient men that he is able to overcome his fear of death. And it is in emulation of those great deeds that he envisions his own great deed of supplanting the imagined republics of the ancient

[47] Leo Strauss, *Natural Right and History* (Chicago: University of Chicago Press, 1953) 251.

world. There is nothing particularly modern about fearing death; it is the human condition. But Machiavelli inaugurates modern philosophy, or at least modern political philosophy, by refusing to accept the human condition, by seeking to conquer death by conquering fortune.

Nietzsche says of Montaigne: "That such a man wrote has truly augmented the joy of living on this earth."[48] Montaigne is a comedian, too, but he laughs at himself; he calls his own life a comedy (I:20,65). It is not too much to say that Montaigne's view is that to philosophize is to learn to live, to have a joyful wisdom concerning the foibles and follies of this world. In the end, he thus appears closer to Saint Francis than to Machiavelli. We should not overlook the similarities between Montaigne and Machiavelli, but neither should we overlook their enormous differences. It is true that both Machiavelli and Montaigne take fortune and death seriously; it is true that both begin something new, using the ancient world as one might use a stepping stone. But when Montaigne insists that he operates "close to the ground" (III:13,849), he in the end appears to repudiate the Machiavellian position from the ground up.

[48] From Nietzsche, "Schopenhauer as Educator," *Untimely Meditations*, 135.

6

Montaigne and Rousseau: Ou, Les Solitaires

Daniel E. Cullen

A comparison of the thought of Montaigne and Rousseau could begin with any one of the numerous and remarkable parallels in the writings of these philosophical autobiographers: the critique of civilization in the name of nature, the loss of freedom in social life, the emphasis on inwardness as the core of selfhood, or the distrust of reason and the appeal to the sentiment of being. But how can one compare two writers who insist so determinedly on their uniqueness? This chapter grapples with this problem, emphasizing the common way in which Montaigne and Rousseau practice philosophy through autobiography. Each writer understands the human problem as the loss of one's natural unity in the agitations of social life. The return to wholeness consequently requires the dissociation of the self from others, and from the accumulated vanities of the soul. Montaigne and Rousseau agree that recovering the sentiment of existence involves a project of self-withdrawal ("*retirer en soi*"). Solitude is the condition of philosophizing in which the soul, freed from its own distractions, "retires" in conversation with itself. But this common recovery project yields significantly different results: for one, a self examined or "essayed;" for the other, the self in reverie, more dependent on imagination and ultimately less self-aware, and less individuated. By the same means, Montaigne and Rousseau arrive at diverse ends.

"I am myself," Montaigne announces, "the matter of my book."(To the Reader, 2)[1] Rousseau's *Confessions* echoes this self-concern: "I wish to show my fellows a man in all the truth of nature, and this man will be myself. Myself alone. (*Moi seul.*)"[2] *The Reveries of the Solitary Walker* returns to the question: "What am I?" posed again in the context of being alone (*seul*)."[3] Each author emphasizes that he writes of himself and for himself alone. Montaigne declares, "If I had written to seek the world's favor, I should have bedecked myself better, and should present myself in a studied posture. I want to be seen here in my simple, natural, ordinary fashion, without straining or artifice; for it is myself that I portray." [4] For his part, Rousseau describes his enterprise as taking the measure of his own soul, acknowledges Montaigne as his predecessor, but claims a different "goal," insisting that he alone truly writes only for himself (To the Reader, 2).[5] But each writer also claims that his singular nature expresses something universal about the

---

[1] Montaigne, *Essays* "To the Reader," 2/3. References to the *Essays* are to Donald Frame's translation: *The Complete Works of Montaigne* (Stanford: Stanford University Press, 1957). Page references to Rousseau's works are first to the five-volume Pléiade edition: *Oeuvres complètes*, Bernard Gagnebin et Marcel Raymond eds. (Paris: Gallimard, 1959, hereafter cited as OC), followed by *The Collected Writings of Rousseau*, eds. Christopher Kelly and Roger Masters (hereafter cited CW).

[2] *Confessions*, OC I, 5/CW V, 5.

[3] *Rêveries*, OC I, 995/CW VIII, 3.

[4] *Essais,9/2* "To the Reader."

[5] *Rêveries*, OC I, 1001–02/CW VIII, 7–8.

human condition; somehow, the particularity of his being discloses the truth of being in general.[6]

The uniqueness of Montaigne and Rousseau's selves can only be revealed in isolation. The recovery of unity or individuality thus involves a movement from society to solitude, reversing the course of Rousseau's natural man. For Montaigne and Rousseau, our nature is such that our happiness consists in living *seul*, and each holds up a mirror to his self in the condition of solitude. [7] Neither, of course, is actually *l'homme isolé*, but each holds that the good life is properly self-centered and private. Montaigne declares: "I have a singular desire that we should each be judged in ourselves apart that I may not be measured in conformity with the common pattern" (I:37,169). The way we live is disordered; social life divides and imprisons the soul. Because we are, in Rousseau's phrase, "everywhere in chains," we must struggle to achieve the solitary condition (I:39,176).[8] But the malaise afflicting social man is more than social: "Our illness grips us by the soul" which is "agitated by diverse passions." Overwhelmed by vanity, our imagination drives us further away from ourselves, preventing us from making a "continuous body out of all this succession of feelings"

---

[6] See *Essays* III:2,611 On Repentance: "Each man bears the entire form of man's estate(*l'humaine condition*)." On Rousseau's life as a paradigm see Michael Davis, *The Autobiography of Philosophy* (Lanham, MD: Rowan and Littlefield Publishers, 1999) 7, 15; and more generally, Christopher Kelly, *Rousseau's Exemplary Life* (Ithaca: Cornell University Press, 1987).

[7] Rousseau opens the *Reveries* with the declaration, "I am now alone on earth, no longer having any brother, neighbor, friend, or society other than myself." *Reveries* OC I, 995/CW, 3. Howsoever natural the solitary condition may be, it remains "strange." Ibid., OC II, 1002/CW, 9.

[8] Cf. Ibid, I:39,176: "We take our chains along with us; our freedom is not complete."

(I:38,173-74). This division or distraction of the self can only be cured by bringing the soul back to itself: by "repossessing" it, as it were.

The trajectory of Montaigne's self-reclamation project has been described by Jean Starobinski in terms of a triple movement that first discovers the self in the world, then retreats from the world and its vanities, and finally reunites with the world in a spirit of acceptance.[9] "Of solitude" demonstrates this complex pattern (I:39).

Montaigne associates solitude with a self-alienation from others and worldly concerns. The dominant theme of the essay is "retirement," and at first Montaigne proposes solitude as the antidote to the pretensions of ambition, and as the natural and inevitable condition of a man who, his powers fading with age, properly withdraws from the realm of action. But retirement is not simply a matter of necessity or prudence; the wise man who, like Montaigne, has the temperament suited to its precepts will *choose* solitude because it is the true condition of our well being (*nostre aise*). Because engagement with others necessarily draws us away from ourselves, self-possession (*avoir soi*) *requires* retirement, for only in that condition can one "concentrate" on oneself (I:39,178).

Social life is the condition of dis-ease; but the illness is in us as well as in our circumstances. Montaigne proposes bringing the soul to rest by withdrawing it into itself and uprooting it from the "popular condition," which is *in* us as well as around us. In ridding ourselves (*desprenons nous*) of all relations that

[9] Jean Starobinski, *Montaigne in Motion,* trans. Arthur Goldhammer (Chicago: University of Chicago Press, 1985) Ch. 2. See also Ann Hartle, *Michel de Montaigne: Accidental Philosopher* (Cambridge: Cambridge University, 2003) 3.

attach us to others, we acquire the power to live truly alone (*à bon escient vivre seuls*) and recover our natural sense of well-being (*aise*). Although the circumstances of social life are alienating, Montaigne emphasizes that our illness in rooted in our soul. Like the dog whose collar remains attached after it has ostensibly broken free, our freedom is not complete (I:39,175-77).

Like Rousseau after him, Montaigne regarded relations to others as a threat to the integrity of the self, but we might find refuge from the gaze of others in our intimate knowledge of ourselves. Echoing Machiavelli's dictum that while many see us, few can touch who we really are, Montaigne writes: "Others see not so much your nature as your art" (III:2,613). Montaigne advises that we manage appearances for others while remaining true to ourselves. Unlike Rousseau however, Montaigne seems to accept that living with reference to others *is* part of our natural condition, and that the art we employ in managing our appearance to them is also part of our nature.[10] But how, Rousseau might ask, can the self remain *free* in the world of others? Montaigne's answer is that the encounter with others is guarded by the fortress of solitude.[11] We must hold back in reserve an aspect of our self that cannot be seized by society. Stated differently: "We must lend ourselves to others [and] give ourselves only to ourselves" (III:10,767).

In "Of Solitude," Montaigne explains: "We must reserve a back shop (*arrière boutique*) all our own, entirely free, in which to establish our real liberty and our principal retreat and solitude." In this refuge, "our ordinary conversation (*entretien*)

[10] See Starobinski, *Montaigne in Motion*, 92, 95.

[11] Hugo Friedrich, *Montaigne* ed. Philippe Desan (Berkeley: University of California Press, 1991) 249.

must be between us and ourselves, and so private that no outside association or communication can find a place; here we must talk and laugh, as if without wife, without children, without possessions." This conversation of the self with the self represents a doubling of existence (as Rousseau will later call it). "We have a soul that can be turned upon itself (*contournable en soy mesme*); it can keep itself company," following the model of the friendship Montaigne experienced with Étienne de la Boétie (I:39,177).

"True solitude" can be enjoyed in the midst of cities and courts but it is enjoyed most conveniently *alone*. In solitude we can be a world to ourselves, but the way we live now is a profound betrayal of that possibility, and of our good; we live and die for "vain considerations." Montaigne writes: "Among our customary actions there is not one in a thousand that concerns ourselves" (I:39,177). According to "Of solitude," we must "break free from the violent clutches that engage us elsewhere and draw us away from ourselves," untie ourselves from society and reunite with ourselves (I:39,178). Montaigne proliferates metaphors of oppression: our soul is burdened with baggage that must be thrown overboard; it is not enough to avoid the crowd: one must escape "the popular condition" that weighs down the soul. We must sequester ourselves in order to repossess ourselves (*r'avoir de soy*), and, finally, we must break the chains we carry with us (I:39,176).

And yet, Montaigne dismisses the life of privation recommended by ancient philosophers and, anticipating Locke's "comfortable self-preservation," defends the commodities of life. Montaigne confesses to having a common soul, incapable of the heroic self-denial of the sages. He warns, as Ann Hartle has observed, against the pretension to divinity or to the angelization of human nature by bringing our attention back to the body and to our common human condition. Rejecting "deliberate philosophy" as a path toward the rule of the soul, Montaigne's thinking departs the common and familiar for the rare and strange, but then returns to find the rare in the common and the strange in the familiar.[12] In this moment of "homecoming," the self experiences the enjoyment of its own being.

Although Montaigne is regarded as a forerunner of liberalism, the characteristic movement of his thought could be described as conservative: the estrangement from the familiar world, and the transcendence of that estrangement culminate finally in the return to the old attachments with a new appreciation, and in a spirit of reconciliation.[13] Montaigne warns that it is especially ambition—what Rousseau would later call *"la fureur de se distinguer"*—that keeps us with the crowd. The souls of the ambitious, brimming with intentions, are too much in the world; to the extent that they step back from it, it is "only to make a better jump." The path of the wise is to "Retire into yourself" (*Retirez vous-en vous*), but one must prepare adequately because it is as possible to fail at solitude as it is to fail at relations with others (I:39,182).

The proper use of solitude is to regain the self-possession that would enable us to resist the tendency of our passions to disperse the self outward. We never feel at home, but always

---

[12] Hartle, *Montaigne*, 7-8.

[13] On Montaigne as a forerunner of liberalism broadly (and philosophically) understood, see the impressive work of David Lewis Schaefer, *The Political Philosophy of Montaigne* (Ithaca: Cornell University Press, 1990) chapters 11-12.

beyond ourselves.[14] The path to self-possession can only be an inward route, leading to the occupation of the self with itself. As Starobinski has remarked, the great paradox is that "it is man's nature to use his reason to contradict or occlude what is given in nature."[15] Nevertheless, Montaigne stops short of arguing for our complete submission to the "authority of Nature."[16]

What way of life, then, emerges from Montaigne's *Essays*?[17] One model evokes an experience of naturalness exemplified by the Brazilian cannibals whom Montaigne notoriously praises for their closeness to nature.[18] Precisely because savage man is prerational, he is incapable of denaturing himself.[19] Montaigne's defense of the cannibals is nevertheless artful and limited; he ultimately rejects "the tyranny of nature" and endorses the free use of reason and judgment in departing from the naturally given.[20] Whereas Rousseau emphasize the unity of natural man, for Montaigne human beings are already doubled

---

14 As Rousseau will later put it: we live "outside ourselves."

15 *Montaigne in Motion*, 215ff.

16 *Essays*, II.8,279: "Since it has pleased God to give us some capacity for reason, so that we should not be, like the animals, slavishly subjected to the common laws, but should apply ourselves to them by judgment and voluntary liberty, we must indeed yield a little to the simple authority of Nature, but not let ourselves be carried way tyrannically by her: reason alone must guide our inclinations." Cf. Rousseau, *Social Contract,* Book I, chapter 8, paragraph 3.

17 The following discussion is heavily indebted to Alan Levine, *Sensual Philosophy: Toleration, Skepticism, and Montaigne's Politics of the Self* (Lanham: Lexington Books, 2001) 89-166.

18 *Essays,* I.31.

19 In the *Discourse on the Origins of Inequality.*

20 See II.16 "Of Glory," 469, and note 28 above, Rousseau develops this point for his own purposes.

or divided within themselves. We can never be as spontaneous as the portrait of savage existence, passively synchronized to the rhythms of nature, suggests. The self is always operating on, and forming itself,[21] but this self-construction must be carefully distinguished from the idea of engineering the self on the basis of reason. Montaigne attributes the latter project to Socrates and criticizes it explicitly. As Starobinski puts it, "The self's action upon itself will be not so much an innovating transformation as a portrait of that which, within us and *despite our will*, is already subject to change, already linked to the general agitation and universal drift of the world."[22] For Montaigne, the formative act is therefore "practically identical with acceptance of oneself (*consentement à soi*). Judgment stands apart from the motives of ordinary life but only in order to see those motives more clearly and to let them emerge with greater freedom."[23]

This complex stance of judgment and acceptance requires an attitude toward the self utterly beyond the capacity of natural man, indicating that the latter cannot be a standard for Montaigne the way he appears to be for Rousseau. Whereas Rousseau could (almost!) declare that "the man who reasons is a depraved animal" (III:6,694), Montaigne ultimately rejects the model of natural life *because* it is unreflective. In the essay, "Of coaches," Montaigne laments that the new world savages were not conquered by the ancient Greeks or Romans, who would have, so to speak, refined and enlarged their natural

[21] Starobinski, *Montaigne in Motion*, 218-19.
[22] Ibid. Emphasis added.
[23] Ibid.

virtues by cultivating the seeds that nature had merely sewn in them.[24]

The natural virtue of the cannibals is fragile because it is unsupported by the faculty of *judgment.* It is their fortunate condition that keeps them simple and free, but that condition is vulnerable to disruption by accident and the shock of the new. The alternative to the savage pattern is not, however, ancient Greek or Roman virtue but Montaigne himself, who exercises reason and judgment, and whose self-possession avoids a corrupting *self-extension.* The self-possession of a Socrates on the battlefield is indeed a better model of human constancy than the naturalness of the savage. The latter is a useful rhetorical device for expounding the human problem, but natural man does not represent its cure because his tranquility of mind is procured without mindfulness.[25] Montaigne's phenomenology of his own judgment reveals a mode of awareness of self that preserves its naturalness while transcending it.

Is there, then, a path to self-possession through self-consciousness that is superior to primitive tranquility and immune to the disruptions of reason? Can there be a free mind that both follows nature and avoids the natural tendencies of the mind itself "to presumption and vanity?"[26] The difficulty is that the mind's faculties are vulnerable to disorder and must be combated even as they are put to use. The harmonious

---

[24] For this interpretation I draw heavily on Levine, *Sensual Philosophy*, ch. 3, especially 111-19.

[25] "Others feel the sweetness of some satisfaction and of prosperity; I feel it as they do, but it is not in passing and slipping by. Instead we must study it, savor it, and *ruminate* it, … . I *meditate* on any satisfaction, I do not skim over it." "Of Experience" *Essays*: III.13, 1092/854 Emphasis added.

[26] See Levine, *Sensual Philosophy*, 122.

condition of natural man was preserved by the boundaries of his pre-rational habits; but what are the preserving limits appropriate to a reflective self? The answer, according to Montaigne, is a skepticism that keeps the essaying self within limits, steering it clear of metaphysical beliefs and pretensions to certitude.

Because the passions disperse the self outward, the route back to self-possession must be inward, toward the occupation of the self with itself; yet what Montaigne discovers in his essaying of himself is not a stable identity but, he says, "a patchwork, and so shapeless and diverse in composition that each bit, each moment, plays its own game. And there is as much difference between us and ourselves as between us and others" (II:1,244). The contrariety of the human self necessitates (or invites) the effort to "probe the inside and discover what springs set men in motion."[27] We must therefore be critical self-seekers, on guard against the unruly aspects of our nature. Like the passions, our mind tends to lead us away from ourselves. Montaigne presents himself as the model of a natural and fully human existence one at home with itself, in the "back shop" where our conversation is only with and for ourselves.

The self in conversation is a metaphor for thinking that implies a division or doubling of the self, but in a unifying rather than alienating way. The soul that can be turned toward itself need not simply turn away from worldly attachments. In calling on us to strip ourselves of our obligations, Montaigne mimics the inhumanity of the Stoic sage: while we will continue to love this or that thing (as we will continue to have wives, children and possessions), we must be *married* only to

[27] II.1, 320/244.

ourselves (I:39,178). But he immediately softens this bracing injunction as follows: let the things of the world be ours, but not so joined to us that they cannot be detached without, so to speak, tearing off our own skin with them. The things of the world, including our relations with others, should be regarded as "accidental commodities" that are external to us (*hors de nous*) and to be used so far as they are pleasing to us. But we should not make of them our principal foundation: "They are not, and neither reason nor nature wills it" (I:39,179). Why should we, Montaigne asks, contrary to the laws of reason and nature subject our happiness to the power of another?

Montaigne cites the Socratic dictum that while the young and mature should devote themselves respectively to education and action, the old should live at their own discretion, without the obligation of office. But that such freedom is not limited to the old is indicated by Montaigne's immediate reference to those temperaments that are more suited to the precepts of retirement than others. His "lassitude," and a will that makes him reluctant to enter the lists, distinguishes Montaigne from those "active and busy" souls who are passionate about all things and are everywhere engaged. Montaigne's "weak or lazy soul" is his by nature *and* by conviction (*discours*). Adverting to those moral prodigies who guard their independence by "excessive virtue," Montaigne gently reproaches their inhumanity: "I am occupied enough without going so far. It is enough for me while enjoying fortune's favor to prepare for its disfavor, and while I am at ease to anticipate the evils that are to come" (I:39,179).

The solitary self will welcome the "commodities" of the world and avoid needless suffering; solitary life, Montaigne assures us, must be "neither laborious nor boring" (I:39,180). One's particular occupation will depend on one's taste, and Montaigne avers that his is not amenable to domestic affairs. But to the extent that it is bound up with a concern for reputation he also criticizes occupying the mind with books, and here one suspects that Montaigne carefully distinguishes himself from the philosophic enterprise generally. The vaunted other-worldliness of the philosopher is belied by the concern for future renown. Montaigne reveals that even the Stoic icon Cicero was too enamored of glory, too solicitous of his reputation. Having mastered his body, his soul remained with the crowd. For his part, Montaigne admits to having a common soul that prefers bodily comfort to spiritual repose. We might say that Montaigne has an uncommon appreciation of the ordinary. Returning to the idea of dialogic friendship with oneself, he warns that one can fail at solitude as at sociability: caution is therefore in order: "You and one companion are an adequate theater for each other, or you for yourself.... We must do like the animals who rub out the tracks at the entrance to their lairs.... Retire into yourself" (I:39,182).

Montaigne's skepticism is deployed against two significant but flawed ways of life: against the life of an overestimated reason that presumes a certainty it does not have, and a life of primitive simplicity that cleaves to the pattern of nature through its self-regulating passions. In Montaigne's highly rhetorical depiction, the cannibals approximate the simplicity and tranquility of the Stoic sage.[28] As Rousseau would later put it, "the savage's mind is undisturbed and given over to the sole sentiment of existence, agitated by nothing."[29] And yet, unlike Rousseau, Montaigne underscores the insufficiency of natural life because it is essentially unreflective.[30] Unsupported by the faculty of judgment, the natural virtue of the cannibals is fragile. In truth, it is their fortunate condition that keeps them simple and free, and that condition is vulnerable to disruption by accident and the shock of the new.[31] Montaigne's natural man enjoyed tranquility of mind but without mindfulness.

Is there, then, a path to self-possession through self-consciousness that, immune to the disruptions of reason, would be superior to savage mindlessness and also associated with philosophical vanity? The alternative to the savage pattern is not some version of ancient virtue but Montaigne himself, who achieves self-possession by exercising his judgment while avoiding reason's corrupting self-extension.[32] The natural, in this view, is both goal and obstacle: the free mind must somehow follow nature, yet avoid the natural tendencies of the mind to presumption, vanity and anxiety.[33]

If the harmonious but imperfect condition of natural man is preserved by the limit of natural custom, what are the preserving limits that corresponds to the reflective self that is consti-tutionally disposed to disregard the naturally given? "We are," Montaigne writes, "I know not how, double within

---

28 See Levine, *Sensual Philosophy,* 107.

29 *Discourse on the Origins of Inequality,* OC III, 144/CW III, 28.

30 "Of Coaches," *Essays,* III:6,694.

31 Levine, *Sensual Philosophy,* 114.

32 Ibid, 116.

33 Ibid, 122; *Essays,* III:12,811.

ourselves, with the result that we do not believe what we believe, and we cannot rid ourselves of what we condemn" (III:12,811). The answer, in short, is Montaigne's particular brand of skepticism that acknowledges limits to the essaying self and guards against the seductions of metaphysics by investigating its own nature.[34] It also guards against the vanity of reason's pretension to rule the soul. Montaigne emphasizes his own soul's vulnerability; he is lucky to have been born with an orderly disposition, for he lacks the firmness of soul to combat disruptive passions. It is Fortune rather than Reason that keeps Montaigne healthy and virtuous.[35] His innocence is childish, "without art;" and yet the self-deprecating Montaigne compares himself favorably to Socrates, who is less spontaneous in ruling his nature on the basis of his reason.[36]

How, finally, are we to accomplish Montaigne's artless or accidental philosophizing? Charles Taylor has argued that Montaigne eschews ontological guarantees of selfhood rooted in either Nature or God, abandoning the vision of a "restored or purified humanity " in favor of an acceptance of limits on the part of the self "returning home."[37] *The Essays* criticize both ancient austerity and Christian asceticism, propounding a new ethos of self-making without ontological commitments. As Taylor states: with Montaigne we no longer try to connect the mind to the order of all things; rather than follow a supposed *telos* of nature, we discover the uniqueness of our own form,

---

[34] Levine, *Sensual Philosophy,* 132.

[35] "Of cruelty," *Essays* II:13,313.

[36] A point emphasized by Ann Hartle in *Michel de Montaigne.*

[37] Charles Taylor, *Sources of the Self: The Making of Modern Identity* (Cambridge: Harvard University Press, 1992) 345-48.

becoming thereby the architects of our own character.[38] Montaigne's vital skepticism sees through vain appearances, and is chastened by the impossibility of "pure vision." But the ontological pessimism instilled by the remoteness of God or the inaccessibility of pure essence is not the last word. The very recognition that we are incapable of penetrating to the hidden essence that would justify our contempt for appearances makes possible in a third move: a return to the phenomenal world in a new spirit of acceptance. Although if our experience must remain individual (rather than universal), it makes possible a feeling of plenitude, that "substitutes for the dispersion of the outside world."[39] As Starobinski explains, once we give up the right to appeal to Being's authority in order to contest the appearances that surround us, we cease to be blinded by presumption and accept that there is no escaping appearances. The recognition that we are always moving from one appearance to the other marks the beginning of an endless discussion of the character of our selfhood, which will not be stabilized in an essential identity.[40]

Rousseau's genetic account of human nature recapitulates the main features of Montaigne's account of the human predicament. The fall from nature into social relations is the general cause of human misery. But the natural state is irretrievable, and Rousseau shows that the equilibrium of power and desire enjoyed by natural man was fortuitous, conditional and consequently fragile.[41] Once expelled by what

---

[38] Ibid, 197.

[39] Starobinski, *Montaigne in Motion*, 93.

[40] Ibid, 85.

[41] Jean-Jacques Rousseau, *Letter to Beaumont, Collected Writings* Vol. 9, ed. Christopher Kelly and Eve Grace, 28-29. (OC IV, 936-37).

Rousseau calls "fatal accidents" from this privileged condition, the self can no longer even recognize its original happiness. In the *Discourse on Inequality*'s grim narrative, civilized humanity loses the sentiment of a free and harmonious existence. But in his autobiographical writings, Rousseau resumes the question whether a non-alienated existence remains available to one who might overcome the corruptions of social life and recover natural sensibility in the experience of interiority. Rousseau's inquiry thus aligns with Montaigne's concern to extricate the self from the thicket of civilizational corruption.

Social man's predicament, according to Rousseau, is that he can no longer regard only himself; unlike natural man, social man is forced to act on principles other than his immediate inclinations, and to consult his reason rather than heed his feelings. The interaction of reason with the passions is inflammatory rather than moderating and generates disorder in the soul. Rousseau had no confidence in the capacity of reason to rule the passions, but he did attribute to the condition of primitive man, a natural equilibrium of power and desire, the structure of which might be reproduced on the plane of social and human existence.[42]

In social circumstances, the only real path to happiness is the path of reason, and here Rousseau seems to agree with Montaigne. Neither proposes a return to the primitive condition of nature, such as that of Montaigne's cannibals; but the equilibrium of our desires and our faculties, which was characteristic of primitive man's unenlightened condition might, in principle, be restored on a new plane. The human dilemma is that in raising ourselves above nature we

[42] I elaborate this argument in *Freedom in Rousseau's Political Philosophy* (DeKalb: Northern Illinois University Press, 1993).

simultaneously fall below it. Becoming human involves the loss of the experience of being oneself; the development of the human faculties and the onset of social relations destroys our self-sufficiency and psychic independence. Social man's existence is external, and his sense of self is mediated by the hostile opinions of others. Can social man recapture any semblance of a healthy individuality? Is it possible for a human being to escape the depraved existence that has become mankind's civilizational fate and live again in harmony with himself? That is Rousseau's question, and we have seen that it is also Montaigne's. But everything hinges on the character of the envisioned harmony, and the way the experience of solitude facilitates it.

As we have seen, for Rousseau, the fatal interaction of passions and reason in the individual—which is later exacerbated by the development of social relations—leaves the self trapped in a disorder from which it cannot extricate itself. The very reason that ought to guide us becomes the instrument of the passions it ought to regulate. The conundrum, then, is that a healthy reason only emerges by the stimulus of unhealthy passion.[43] Is there an intermediary form of existence between the healthy (but not fully human) natural man and the diseased civilized man?

Both Montaigne and Rousseau draw attention to the false appearances of the world, to the superiority (and fragility) of the natural, and to the tendency of reason to draw us away from rather than toward ourselves. Because he is more skeptical than Rousseau about the goodness of nature and the weakness

[43] For this analysis see Jean-Marie Salien, "Dialectique de la Raison et des Passions Dans la Pensée de Jean-Jacques Rousseau," *12 International Studies in Philosophy*, 1980.

of reason, the reconciliation or "homecoming of the self that Montaigne offers a more plausible alternative to our distracted consciousness than Rousseau's vision of a restored human wholeness. Whereas Montaigne regards the condition of self-division as a consequence of our variable nature and as an opportunity for self-development, Rousseau views man's "perfectibility" as a catastrophe. For Rousseau the divided self is the worst condition of humanity, but the inner division of which Montaigne writes is what opens the space for judgment. The result is not an alienating inner conflict, but a ratification of the passions that happens to also check their impetuosity.[44]

To be sure, Montaigne leaves us with a paradoxical account of a judgment that both does and does not transform the self. What Montaigne discovers in the essaying of his own self is not a stable unity but a "patchwork." As Starobinski observes, one paradox of the *Essays* as a book is the way it conveys a sense of unity to Montaigne's life even as it catelogues the natural inconstancy of Montaigne's self. The self-awareness of Montaigne's reflection is distinguishable both from the cannibal's unreflective naturalness and Socrates' rational mastery of his soul. Montaigne writes in the final essay, "Of experience:" "Do I find myself in some tranquil state? Is there some voluptuous pleasure that tickles me? I do not let my sense pilfer it, I bring my soul into it, not to implicate herself, but to enjoy herself, not to lose herself but to find herself" (III:13,854). This is a form of judgment and a level of self-awareness, which the natural man can never attain. This exquisite form of self-preservation combines self-love and self-knowledge, not in the pursuit of some ontological unity, but in

[44] Starobinski, *Montaigne in Motion*, 220, n.22.

the acceptance of our inner dividedness. Self-conscious life involves a standing back from one's interests and feelings in a posture of judgment and development or cultivation. One can construct broader interests and conceive projects that integrate the various moments of experience.

Montaigne accepts that the experience of our interiority is always imperiled as the reason of its own being eludes the inconstant self. The skeptical subject must find its meaning and secure its preservation in the absence of ontological foundations. The greatest paradox is that self-knowledge becomes both necessary and possible only by renouncing the aspiration to knowledge of the whole. The self to be known stands equally apart from Nature and God.[45]

What seems missing, by contrast, in Rousseau's account of self-hood is the constructive project at the center of Montaigne's enterprise. If the experience of self-division in which man constitutes himself as both subject and object is the peculiarly modern way of self-consciousness, Rousseau appears to resist it.[46] Rather than essaying the dialogic self, Rousseau imagines abolishing the inner division. Rousseau could never endorse Montaigne's conclusion: "Painting myself for others, I have painted my inward self with colors clearer than my original ones" (II:18,504).[47] Montaigne cannot know himself outside his autobiography; it is literally a process of self-

[45] See Dieter Henrich, "The Basic Structure of Modern Philosophy" 2 *Cultural Hermeneutics* 1984, 1-18.

[46] See Michael Gillespie, "Montaigne's Humanistic Liberalism," 47 *The Journal of Politics 1985,* 147.

[47] Cf Gillespie, "Montaigne's Humanistic Liberalism," 148.

composition, which involves him in modeling, fashioning and revising himself for his own understanding.[48]

In Rousseau's genealogy of human *dis-ease*, from the onset of social relations, the soul is victimized, its natural *amour de soi* displaced by *amour propre*. Describing the natural man as *l'homme isolé*, Rousseau first portrays the condition of solitude in terms of an immunity from other wills. One can find similar notions in Montaigne, but the latter also offers a positive argument for solitude. It is because we have "*une âme contournable en soys-meme*"—a soul capable of bending toward itself—that allows a dialogue and friendship with oneself is possible. This dialogic self is, I suggest, a more human and more philosophic possibility than Rousseau's parallel *rentrer en soi-même*, which appears to thrust the self back to a pre-conscious level of existence. The doubling of the self Montaigne describes is not subject to the pain of division described by Rousseau; and the self's indeterminacy is likewise less a threat than an invitation to exploration.[49]

In the *Reveries*, Rousseau seems to deliberately echo Montaigne's account of solitude, including the fact that his solution permits him to converse with his soul, to give a "shapeless" account of himself, and to examine the succession of his adventitious feelings and thoughts.[50] But, whereas for Montaigne, solitude was the achievement of a determined soul, Rousseau attributes his isolation to the malevolence of other men. Rousseau describes himself as "forced" to reflect on his dispositions. Ironically, his self-knowledge is the unintended consequence of their malevolence. In the "Second Walk"

---

[48] Ibid.

[49] Cf. Davis, *Autobiography*, 76.

[50] *Rêveries* OC I, 999/CW V, 6.

Rousseau suggests that his solitude (albeit imposed on him by men) is the fulfillment of nature's intention, the condition in which he is fully himself "without diversion and without obstacle."[51]

Rousseau's "Moral Letters" express so many of the themes of Montaigne's "Solitude" that one imagines him having the *Essays* at hand.[52] But his most remarkable statement is that philosophy is not the means to self-knowledge; rather, one must first "return to oneself" in order to philosophize.[53] As Christopher Kelly has remarked, Rousseau challenges the status of philosophy: "genuine philosophy is the result of a prior turning inward, but it does not bring about the turning inward."[54] Rousseau refers repeatedly to "gathering oneself together" (*receuillir*) but does he collect himself in thought, or does he lose himself in reverie?[55] In the second Letter to Malsherbes, Rousseau describes how his detachment from society inspired him to create another one in his imagination, to which he could repair without effort and without disappointment. By means of the chimeras he creates, Rousseau

---

[51] Ibid, OC II, 1002/CW V, 9.

[52] "Let us begin by becoming ourselves again, by centering ourselves in ourselves, by circumscribing our soul with the same limits that nature has given to our being;"…"The first idea of man is to separate himself from everything that is not his himself;"…"commune with yourself , seek out solitude;"…"The solitude in question…is to take your soul out of the throng." Rousseau, "Moral Letters" 6, in *Rousseau on Philosophy, Morality and Religion* ed. Christopher Kelly (Hanover: Dartmouth College Press, 2007) 96-97. Rousseau even refers to "obtaining your own friendship with yourself" in solitude. Ibid, 99.

[53] Ibid, 97.

[54] Ibid, xxvi.

[55] See Davis, *Autobiography*, 119.

is now the author of his own happiness. He fills the universe with himself.[56]

Rousseau's propensity for becoming "lost in thought" raises a profound question about the status of thinking itself:[57] how does the activity of philosophy help or hinder the goal of "being restored to oneself?" As Kelly suggests, Rousseau ranks philosophy (and perhaps self-awareness simply) below the sentiment of existence, and perhaps below the "almost automatic life" of those who remain close to nature.[58] In his third *Letter to Malsherbes*, Rousseau answers the question: "What did I enjoy when I was alone? Myself, the whole universe, everything that is, everything that can be, everything that is beautiful in the perceptible world and that is imaginable in the intellectual one."[59] The enjoyment turns out however, to be mediated by memory, causing one to wonder whether the experience nature of unfolding itself before Rousseau is a matter of contemplation or dreaming. Rousseau explains that in the enjoyment of solitude "I did not think, I did not reason, I did not philosophize.... I loved to lose myself in imagination in space;... I would have loved to throw myself into the infinite."[60]

---

[56] Letter to Malsherbes, in Kelly ed., *Rousseau on Philosophy*, 151. Cf. Christopher Kelly *Rousseau as Author: Consecrating One's Life to the Truth* (Chicago: University of Chicago Press, 2003) 162-72.

[57] See Kelly, *Rousseau on Philosophy*, xxvii: who notes that in his peak experience Rousseau appears to abandon philosophy and even thought, for a deeper satisfaction. See also Kelly, *Rousseau as Author*, 172-82 for an important treatment of the status of philosophy and contemplation in Rousseau.

[58] Ibid, 177. "Contemplation, as Rousseau liked to practice it, resembles more an aesthetic activity than a philosophic one." Ibid, 179.

[59] Kelly, *Rousseau on Philosophy*, 154.

[60] Ibid, 156.

Let us acknowledge that losing oneself is quite different from secluding oneself in the *arrière-boutique*, or covering one's tracks to the lair. Rousseau understands his "retreat" as a consequence of exile rather than choice. It was the fortuitous choice of others that permitted him to return to himself and rediscover his natural inclinations. What then, finally, is the character of Rousseau's solitary life? What purpose does his solitude serve? To be the author of one's being is to reconstruct or recollect experiences of satisfaction, which cannot now be experienced except through the mediation of thought. As the account of his accident in "Second Walk" (*Reveries*) suggests, unconscious-ness, or the pleasing gap between consciousness and awareness is the peak experience for Rousseau. Reverie is Rousseau's term for this way station between non-being and being.[61]

Montaigne's self-authorship seems, by comparison, more active and constructive. To *essay* the self is to embrace the double character of consciousness; the irony of self-knowledge consists in the alienation required by the thinking soul. "To be human is to be two."[62] Perhaps the chief difference between the uses of solitude in Montaigne and Rousseau is that Rousseau seeks refuge in the imagination, retreating to an alternative world that is immune to the instabilities of real life, whereas Montaigne's "back shop" is a haven within the world.[63] The

---

[61] Davis, Autobiography, 129. See also the brilliant discussion of Rousseau and Montaigne and their "near death" experiences in Pierre Munent, "Montaigne and Rousseau: Some Reflections" in Christopher Kelly and Eve Grace ed., *The Challenge of Rousseau* (Cambridge: Cambridge University Press, 2012).

[62] Ibid, 132.

[63] On the superiority of the imagination in Rousseau's calculus, see Kelly, *Rousseau's Exemplary Life,* 230, and 232-33.

essaying self cannot remain in a state of idleness or self-absorption for long; to take the measure of one's soul one must make tracks, and venture outside the lair.

Index